The Top 100 Questions

REMIX

Richard Bewes
Edited by Ian Thompson

Scripture Quotations marked (NIV) are from *The Holy Bible, New International Version*. Copyright ©1973, 1978, 1984, by International Bible Society. Used by permission of Hodder and Stoughton, a memeber of the Hodder Headline Group. All rights reserved. 'NIV' is a regirstered trademark of International Bible Society. UK trademark number 1448790.

Scripture Quotations marked (ESV) are from *The Holy Bible, English Standard Version*, published by HarperCollins Publishers ©2001 by Crossway Bibles, a division of Good News Publishers. Used by permission. All Rights Reserved.

Scripture Quotations marked (KJV) are from the King James Version Bible.

ISBN 1-84550-191-8
ISBN 978-1-84550-191-4

© Copyright Richard Bewes 2006

10 9 8 7 6 5 4 3 2 1

Based on *The Top 100 Questions*
by Richard Bewes first published in 2002
This edition first published in 2006
by
Christian Focus Publications, Ltd
Geanies House, Fearn, Tain,
Ross-shire, IV20 1TW, Great Britain.

www.christianfocus.com

Cover Design by Alister MacInnes

Printed and bound by
J. H. Haynes, Sparkford

CONTENTS

INTRODUCTION

If you want to apply the truth of the Bible to our modern, questioning world then you are going to be asked questions. Some may be sarcastic but most will be from people who beneath the surface want answers! The questions and answers that feature in these pages are drawn from those people have asked at public meetings, in a syndicated newspaper column I used to run, late-night conversations, youth events, dinner parties, radio phone-ins, letters from enquirers and innumerable encounters at the church door.

Here now is what I am submitting as *the top hundred* that seem to be surfacing in our twenty-first century. I must declare that this book in no way attempts to present a systematic teaching manual. These are simply answers to questions I have been asked. Nevertheless, by dividing these pages into several sections, we can together cover a fair range of life, belief and experiences that provoke us into asking 'Why?' 'What?' and 'How?'

These are not Bible studies, they are the sort of thing you can say to start a conversation. If it leads to study, great, but we need to be able to show that we have answers that are worth exploring before someone will take us seriously enough to come along.

As far as Bible passages that I quote, I shall use a variety of available versions, including the King James Version (KJV) and the English Standard Version (ESV). **Please look up the references** where space forbids me to make the Bible quotation in full.

I am grateful to those who kindly endorse this book with their generous comments. I am also grateful to my secretary, Miranda Lewis, and our Resource and Communications Co-ordinator, Pam Glover, for their great help while this book has been in preparation. And I am *always* grateful to Anne Norrie and my ever-patient publishers at Christian Focus.

Richard Bewes

Written at All Souls Church, Langham Place, London

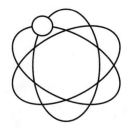

PART ONE
THE UNIVERSE WE INHABIT

'And God saw that it was good'. In these words we see the approval of God stamped upon his work. For God did not merely discover that his work was good after he had finished it, but he teaches us that it is good...There cannot be a higher author, a more effectual instrument, or a more excellent reason, than God, his Word, and his creation of the good.'

The City of God
Augustine of Hippo AD354–430

Q.1

One universe or many?

Is Jesus Christ 'IT' or is he only part of something yet bigger still? Are there other systems out there, alien to our own?'

The answer to the question lies in just whom exactly Jesus Christ is. He is the key to the whole of our existence. The Christian apostle Paul sums up the divine purpose in vivid language: '...to bring all things in heaven and on earth together under one head, even Christ' (Eph. 1:10).

Why a universe, and not a series of 'multi-verses'? Christ is the single, unifying reason. As two student leaders – Tom Parsons and Stephen Nichols – once explained in a Bible study at All Souls Church in London, 'Even the origin of the word university (Latin: 'uni' – one; 'veritas' – truth) reflects the vision of a single coherent story, one truth. From the beginning, all subjects in our campuses – physics, music or mathematics – were separate chapters in one over-arching story, slices cut from one cake.'

But in recent years the widespread loss of confidence in there being just one true story has resulted in a growing collection of highly diverse and irreconcilable 'stories'; there are as many stories as there are story-tellers – 'my' story, 'your' story, the Marxist story, the feminist story. The university curriculum has widened to bizarre dimensions. 'You can even do courses in Star Trek', say Tom and Stephen, 'or studies on the career of some football star!' The idea that there could be one story that explains all the rest – a single factor, an individual Person – is dismissed as naïve.

But this is nothing new. The first Christians were up against the most fragmented world-view imaginable. There was Delphi with its oracle, the rites of the Egyptian god Isis, and Cybele, the mother of gods in Asia. Romans could go to Greece and identify their own Jupiter with Zeus, or visit Syria and find him in Baal. Yet this whole edifice was to crumble.

As the message of Christ took hold – by whose 'blood' all things on earth or in heaven could be made one (Col. 1:20) – a new and unprecedented unity of thought began to take over. Tatian, the second century Christian leader, spoke of the relief of exchanging the tyranny of 10,000 gods for the benign monarchy of one.

Augustine, two centuries later put it like this, 'This Child of the manger fills the world.'

The apostle Paul put it still more dramatically: 'He who descended is the very one who ascended higher than all the heavens, in order to fill the whole universe' (Eph. 4:10). By this Paul meant that -

1] There is no part of the universe that is free from Christ's control.
2] There is no room for anyone else. Diana, Mithras, Jupiter, Osiris and Venus had to go. Jesus has taken all the space!
3] The ascension of Jesus implies, not a Christ-deserted world, but a Christ-filled world.

There is just one great universe – and Christ is its explanation and goal.

Q.2

Are we on our own?

Gyorgy Mandics, a UFO expert from Timisoara in Romania, was reported to have learnt 17 foreign languages, in the hope that he could speak to any aliens who might land on earth. 'I'm sure', he said, 'that aliens exist, and I will be one of the few people able to communicate with them when they arrive'

(London *Metro,* 15 June 2001).

But no such arrival will take place, because aliens do not exist (Wow – big claim!), Gyorgy could have spared himself the trouble. However fascinating the information that comes to us from the scientific exploration of the universe, our scientists could save themselves a great deal of nail-biting suspense, and perhaps money, if they realised that the possibility of alien life is zilch. *We are alone in the universe.* But why can we be so sure on this issue?

The answer is found in a biblical world-view. At the centre of all existence is the one true God, who has focused his loving purposes upon the apex of his created universe – a race of beings, made in his image, and made for fellowship with him. Planet Earth was to be the focal point of God's work. There, we could worship, love, create and govern. To us was entrusted the care of the world and all that was in it (Gen. 1:27,28). So when we, as creation's chief actor, led by the original first couple, fell into rebellion against God, the entire cosmos was affected and remains in a state of discordant tension, 'groaning' to this day (Rom. 8:19-22).

Is there another 'system' outside of ours; another race of beings which, perhaps, has never sinned and doesn't need salvation? No, the destiny of the solitary universe was completely bound up with the human race – a one-off group of beings created with God-like moral responsibility. As custodians, we stood alone. *When we fell, everything else shuddered.* This means that an alien would also be affected by sin and so need saving too.

But there is no Alien Christ. All creation waits – along with us – for the final day of redemption through Christ (Rom. 8:19).

It's Christ, the second Person of the eternal Trinity, who clinches the issue. Coming as God, to be born into our world as a human being, and to save the world through his death as a human being, he cannot pay for the sins of non-humans as he is 'fully human'. Now he is at the right hand of God the Father. There he rules at the centre of everything, as representative of all humanity – not as a resurrected spirit but in a glorified body; not as an *ex-man* but as true and perfect Man, on behalf of his redeemed church.

Here is a consistent, unified picture. What of alien beings, then? They're not in the frame at all. In the Scriptures we learn of angels, but they are not aliens; they are an integral part of the created order, and have a part to play as God's messengers and servants.

It's official, then. Apart from the loving presence of God himself and his servants, we are on our own in the universe.

Q.3

Dwarfed by the distances?

Earth: 'a medium–sized planet, orbiting round an average star in the outer suburbs of an ordinary spiral galaxy, which is itself only one of about a million million galaxies in the observable universe. Yet the strong anthropic* principle would claim that this whole vast construction exists simply for our sake. This is very hard to believe.'

(Stephen Hawking, *A Brief History of Time*, Bantam Press)

Hard to believe? It's impossible to believe if it wasn't for the authoritative witness of the Biblical record that can stand all our historical and scientific probing and endure the test of time.

It is the Bible that gives us a proper perspective and adds new dimensions to Stephen Hawking's world-view without taking anything away from his academic brilliance. Omitted from Hawking's statement are three factors – all of which are vital to the argument.

First, there is the factor of **God**-centredness, not **man**-centredness, in all of our fantastic universe.

Secondly, Hawking omitted to recognise that Creation is the home, not just of the human species as such, *but of a race of God-like beings.* That is our calling, and there is none higher. Thirdly, we must not forget that the whole of Creation centres in a man who, in the New Testament, is described in these terms:

> He is the image of the invisible God, the heir over all creation. For by him
> all things were created: things in heaven and on earth, visible and invisible,
> whether thrones or powers or rulers or authorities; all things were created by
> him and for him. He is before all things, and in him all things hold together
> (Col. 1:15-17)

Here we discover that the universe was created for Jesus Christ, someone who's both God and human, representing the prototype human being. It is only when we bring him into the picture that the fact we live in immense cosmic surroundings begins to lose its weirdness.

Science has tended to point to the stages following the original 'big bang' – in the formation of continents, oceans, vegetation and the animal kingdom – as taking place over many millions of years. So vast are the figures, that our own significance and comparatively short history are reduced virtually to vanishing point.

But the Bible reverses that proportion and turns it round completely.

'The forming of the continents? The tortuous procedures, the millions of years that are said to lie behind those first jellies, crustaceans, and mosses? Dinosaurs and crocodiles? All in a week's work – that's all! We'll give that bit a page – well, perhaps two pages!'

'But for the *real* story; God's plan and focus through people, and his mission to the humans on earth that those experts of yours that dismiss as a perfunctory blip? Why, we'll need something like a thousand pages before we're through!'

It's this perspective that we get from the divine word that puts the balance straight and gives us a better perspective – *and makes our world view bigger.*

* everything revolves around mankind

FOR FURTHER STUDY of our human beginnings, see **Genesis** in the *Book by Book* video studies, with guest contributor Anne Graham Lotz. Enquiries: vestry@allsouls.org (for USA, www.visionvideo.com).

Q.4

Who are we? What are we?

The following statement was made by the Rev. Don Cupitt, a liberal clergyman and theologian who had ceased to believe in the objective reality of God, 'My self is a mere temporary aggregation of processes', he wrote. 'My own desires are part of the flux of forces in nature.'

(From Scott Cowdell's *'Atheist Priest?'*, SCM Press)

Well, try telling that to the judge when you are up on a criminal charge? That, after all, you were no more than a collection of biochemical reactions and that he, too, is another such collection. See what happens! In a world where people are generally held responsible for their actions, the dogged attempts to interpret all wrong-doing as somehow derived from our genes – or as a kind of treatable disease – look pathetically shallow.

There is in every human being an element that says *I know that this is what I want to do but I also know what I should do instead.* This is part of the image of God created in humanity from the beginning:

So God created man in his own image, in the image of God he created him; male and female he created them (Gen. 1:27).

Genesis introduces us to the personal God of spirituality and relationship. It is impossible to understand ourselves as people, without this divine backcloth. True, like the animals we are creatures of common chemicals – we come from the 'dust' (Gen. 2:7) – but 'the breath of life' was breathed into us in a way that seems to be different from the animal kingdom. Genesis 2:7 helps explain Genesis 1:27. In every person there is a spiritual capacity for worship, prayer, and being responsible for what we do. It is this truth that explains not only what we are, but *who* we are.

We are placed above the animals, and in charge of them, not because we are the dominant species, but as managers of the earth's resources – naming and categorising the species (the beginning of zoology and science; Gen. 2:19,20).

We are in the image of God with a spiritual nature – but we are only images! *We are not God himself;* we exist because he made us. In this we are unlike Jesus Christ who is the 'exact' replica of God (Col. 1:15).

This is why New Age teaching eventually fails. It is of little use telling people in their seminars that they 'have a god within' and that there's nothing that they cannot do. Within six months they will discover that they have deadlines to chase, targets to achieve – and ulcers – and that it's obvious that they are *not* God!

Nevertheless, every human being possesses something of the divine **image** in them. It is this that explains generosity, courage or selflessness, even among the irreligious. Anthropologists have used terms such as *homo sapiens* and *homo erectus* to describe humanity. It was my longstanding neighbour of many years, Dr. John Stott, who coined the title *homo divinus.* That divine image has been there from the beginning – albeit severely defaced since humanity's rebellion (see chs. 6 and 7).

FOR FURTHER STUDY: *Open Home, Open Bible* video/DVD series, cassette 6, programme 1. Enquiries: vestry@allsouls.org (for USA, www. visionvideo.com).

Q.5

A woman's place?

Why was the first woman created second, as only a 'helper' for the man? This seems to place women on a lower footing altogether.

Let's be careful, as we look at the Genesis account of our beginnings, not to be tied up either by the order of the words or unthinking literalism. Actually, it's Genesis 1:27 that gives us the definitive answer – where the man and the woman counter-balance each other, side by side:

> So God created man in his own image, in the image of God he created him; male and female he created them.

The account of chapter 1 is filled out and made clear by the details of chapter 2. If we are made in the image of God – who is a Trinity of people in **community** – that will have an effect on us: *'It is not good for the man to be alone. I will make a helper suitable for him'* (Gen. 2:18). It is not 'singleness' that is not good, but *solitude,* or loneliness.

1. The founding principle
There it is, in verse 18. Does 'helper' suggest a lower rank, with Adam as the Skipper of the ship and Eve as a sort of First Mate? Not if you check through a Bible concordance. The majority of Bible references where the same Hebrew word for helper, *ezer,* occurs are used to describe the kind of 'help' that only *God* can give (eg 1 Sam. 7:12; Ps. 121:2; Hosea 13:9).

So Eve, far from being an 'assistant' is actually necessary to make mankind complete. She represents the vital and astounding God-given dimension that we can only call **'otherness'**. George Gilder has written, 'The differences between the sexes are the single most important fact of human society' (*Sexual Suicide,* Bantam, 1973, p.63).

2. The crowning mystery

After Adam has gave names to all the animals he is then introduced to 'the woman'. At this point he does not get out his notebook and exclaim, 'A new species! What shall we call it?' No, this is the electric moment of recognising his other half! The love poem that follows is surely the first in all history (Gen. 2:23).

So Eve is not taken out of 'the ground' – thus forming a new and separate kind of being. She is taken out of Adam's side, because men and women were to be of the very same essence. Exactly how the divine operation was performed we shall never know because Adam was unconscious while it was happening!

3. The defining charter

Look now at Genesis 2:24: *For this reason a man will leave his father and mother and be united to his wife, and they will become one flesh.* This is the creational partnership of **marriage,** endorsed for all time by Jesus (Matt. 19:5), in which members of the two sexes can find intimacy and union, matched *with,* not *against,* each other as life partners (see ch. 73).

Human life should never consist in a battle of the sexes. Christian marriage is to be an illustration of mutual submission, one to the other (Eph. 5:21).

Q.6

Can you explain evil?

I get so discouraged by the evil I see on every side; wars around the world and fights in my street; people out of control on Saturday nights; corrupt leadership in politics and business; terrorism. Why is it always there? Where does it come from? Can I hope for better times?

In spite of everything that we see, there is hope! But the place to look for the answer is in the Scriptures. Here are the briefest of guidelines:

1. Evil represents a defect from perfection

Originally there was God and his goodness. Evil is an intrusion into the universe resulting from *an angelic rebellion,* under a created angel, who aspired to be God himself (Isa. 14:12-15; Ezek. 28:11-19). This co-incided with *humanity's bid for independence,* as expressed by our spiritual ancestors, Adam and Eve (Gen. 3). These two acts of rebellion are part of one and the same act we call *The Fall.*

Fellowship with the Creator was never something that could be programmed or enforced; if you are free to love, then you are also free to rebel. So evil entered not as something that had always existed, but as a deviation, a rebellion from what originally existed.

Augustine wrote:

> The evil angels, though created good, became evil by their voluntary defection from the good, so that the cause of evil is not the good, but defection from the good. (*The City of God,* Book 12)

2. Evil is headed by an imposter, someone who doesn't really control things

Satan, who has a variety of names, is not an 'absolute' being. He is neither all-powerful, all-knowing, nor all-present. The opposite to Satan is not God but

Michael, leader of the angelic hosts (Rev. 12:7). Satan is a rebel and an imitator. 'Satan's purpose', wrote Billy Graham, 'was not to make Eve as ungodly as possible, but to make her as godlike as possible – without God' (*Approaching Hoofbeats,* Word, p.105). As a created being, then, the Devil had a beginning, and he will have an end (Rev. 20:10).

3. Evil produces dullness, not creativity

Genesis 3:14-19 tells us about the entry of evil into the world in terms of dust, death, pain, thorns and thistles. Our whole environment – which we have been told to look after – is affected (Rom. 8:19,20). Because evil lacks the spark of original creativity it can ultimately produce only a desert – a 'ground zero' wasteland. When education, medicine, politics and the arts ignore God, you can expect decline and confusion.

4. Evil ends in defeat, not triumph

The whisper of evil's downfall is already there in Genesis 3:15, where God announces to the serpent of *enmity* [opposition] between the woman's future offspring and his own. The woman's 'offspring' is not plural, but singular – one Person! '**He** will crush your head' (a picture of defeat), 'and you will bruise his heel' (KJV). Even then, the serpent would only be *permitted* to bruise [cause hurt to] Christ only so far as 'it pleased the Lord to bruise him' (Isa. 53:10). The cross would ultimately ensure evil's defeat.

Be encouraged. History and the future belong to a re-establishment of hope!

Q.7

Why am I stuck with Adam?

I don't see why we must all be branded as sinners as a result of a mythical action by two people. I have nothing to do with Adam and Eve.

This was put to me during a phone-in programme. It's important to question the use of the word *mythical.* The New Testament shows us that Jesus believed in the existence of Adam and Eve (eg Matt. 19:4). Also, without what happened in Genesis 3, we would be baffled as to how we got from harmonious innocence in chapter 2 to murderous hatred in chapter 4; and the growing crescendo of evil that followed.

We cannot pretend that nothing had happened. Some have spoken of the Fall as though it was a step *upwards,* as Adam and Eve 'decided for themselves' so it was a mark of 'maturity'. But no; here was a decision – not between good and evil (for they didn't know what evil was), but rather between themselves and God. In the wake of this decision came death, disturbance and disintegration – and all of us are involved.

It was a real choice. If we complain that they should not have been created with the capacity to choose, we are really asking that they should have been created as plants or animals, because the fellowship with God that we were created for would not be fellowship at all, if it can be programmed into us.

Then we have to remind ourselves that Adam and Eve were not simply the first humans; they were *prototype* humans. You can make jelly for a children's party by pouring it into a mould, for it to cool. Every jelly that results will have the same shape. If, of course, you drop the mould and it becomes dented, all the jellies from then on will show up the flaw. *So with the first pair of humans.* The image of God is still there, but it is flawed and dented, right through the entire race, universally.

So, you don't want to be associated with Adam and Eve? **That is good news.** According to the Bible, there are only two representative characters you can be identified with; one is Adam, the other is Jesus Christ – who is the 'second Adam' (Rom. 5: 12-16):

> Just as the result of one trespass was condemnation for all, so also the result of one act of righteousness was justification that brings life for all (v16).

Certainly we can't say that the sin in the Garden had nothing to do with us and it wasn't our fault, because we weren't there. The truth is, we were there! Adam and Eve represent us all. But the other side is seen in the words of the old spiritual: *Were YOU there, when they crucified my Lord?* And the forgiven believer says, 'Yes! I was there. My sins – in which I have consistently followed in the footsteps of Adam – were dealt with at the Cross... and from now on I am part of a second race. I am bound up now with *Christ*'.

Q.8

Extra-terrestrial beings?

How seriously should we regard the theories that God was an astronaut, and that what Ezekiel saw in chapter 1 of his prophecy was a spacecraft?

As a start, please look back at chapter 2. The possibility of UFO's *is* an area of fascination and speculation – and commercialism too! This field of interest drew in many followers with the publication in the last century of such books as von Daniken's *Chariot of the Gods?* This, and a forest of other speculative books, television programmes and Internet web sites, exclusively devoted to the topic, have successfully turned the UFO dream into an *industry*.

Are we surprised? We should not be. For years Marshall MacLuhan, back in the 1950s and 1960s, was forecasting a reaction to the cold, bare landscape presented by 'Modernity' – with its earthbound view that 'all I can see and touch is all that there is'. The sky was closed off, and humanity put itself in a cynical straitjacket.

The next era, he said, would be 'religious'. And while 'scientism' [having science as your God] and the constricted greyness of modernity are still in evidence, 'Post-modernity' has lifted the lid off our world with an array of differing viewpoints and interpretations of life. It has affected architecture, fashion, the arts, music and, of course, people's view of what might be 'out there'. *There are no restrictions!*

The space-craft theory of Ezekiel reveals an interesting mindset. The throne on which the Son of Man is sitting (Ezek. 1:26) is said to be the pilot's seat.

As we have seen, materialism alone has failed to satisfy people, they yearn for 'something beyond', and here is a world-view that lifts readers to dimensions and hopeful possibilities beyond their present horizons. It is also presented in a way that will attract school children, PhDs and lorry drivers alike. It is also undemanding: there is no cost or effort involved in following the gospel of space-fiction. Your intellect is tickled, your hopes are vaguely raised, no moral choices are involved and no adjustment to your lifestyle is called for.

Christians should reach out with warmth – but with truth – towards the advocates for extra-terrestrial beings. *'You're onto something!'* should be our reaction. *'There IS another dimension above and beyond what we can see around us. The feeling that 'The Truth is Out There' just might be a first stepping stone to finding the source of all truth!'*

And then we should begin to point to God, the only true God, who is behind the visions and super-normal appearances featured in the Bible. But he is a God who presents us with the supreme adventure of becoming members of a City that is going to last for ever. And it is a City that will descend upon us, from above, historically, right here upon Planet Earth. Turn with them to Revelation 21:2...and they'll see. We must *all* get ready!

Q.9

The creation of viruses?

If God created all things, why did he create terrible things like viruses?

All forms of life would originally have been perfect: let's understand that straight away. Even today some bacteria are positively beneficial, people drink little pots of yoghurt every day or take things to aid their digestion – these are no more nor less than 'friendly' forms of bacteria. We would not be able to digest our food properly without some of them in our gut.

In the background of any discussion around the question we need to understand that since the fall of humanity; disease, decay and death have broken in on our existence. We have only to read, in Genesis chapter 5, the repeated use of the phrase *'and then he died'* to take in the inevitability of death, and its causes. Viruses are part of this revised world order. What can we learn from them?

1. They make us humble

Long before the electron microscope had identified the virus, the very presence of disease and infection was a constant reminder that we are subject to death. None of us escapes; in a hundred years or so there's a clean sweep right across the planet of everyone. Certainly the answer has been found to some of these viruses, but there is no denying that, however long we live, it is usually some infection that finally kills us. But consider this too:

2. They make us think of eternity

A virus attack will cause us to look up and around for answers. This heightens the possibility of our becoming exposed to the one factor that can give us real guidance – the revelation that God has given us in the Bible that leads us to the answer offered by Jesus Christ. Many millions of people never even began to think about God and his saving plan until they, or a loved one, were struck by an apparently random disease.

Focus on the virus alone and the mystery may seem not to have a solution but the virus is part of a bigger picture. If we can stand a little further back, we can see that the virus is part of the 'fallenness' of our situation and that the wide-angle lens of God's revelation let's us see how God's loving purposes can restore this world to a better place.

3. They help us identify with fellow humans

If God declared war on evil, pain and death – and he has clearly done so in Christ – then we must allow the presence of such infection and disease to provoke us into fighting them in his name. When I was a boy growing up in Africa; poliomyelitis was feared. How thankful we should be that there were researchers dedicated to ridding the world of this and other viruses. Christians can, and should, stand in firm support of them, with love as our motivation, and the resurrection as our confidence.

Q.10

Where do animals fit in?

What is the purpose of animals in our world? How do they compare to humans?

Despite the love of many for animals, thinking people have tended to make them less important in the divine scheme of things. This may partly be due to the influence wielded by Aristotle, the Greek philosopher and scientist (384–322 BC). He regarded animals as virtually on the same level as plants – and his thinking has left its stamp upon the western world.

But it may be said of animals that, like humanity, they too were endowed with 'the breath of life' (Gen. 6:17), although not reflecting God's image like us. Great emphasis is given in Genesis chapters 6–9 to God's regard for the animals that were created in their magnificent variety. Their relationship to the Creator is highlighted in the psalmist's celebration of creation (Ps. 104). This is a planet teeming with wild life of every kind whose protection and conservation is part of God's command to the human race as given to Adam and all his successors.

After the Flood, God established his covenant with Noah, his descendants and with 'the birds, the livestock and all the wild animals... every living creature on earth' (Gen. 9:8-11).

We would not be able to get along in life without the aid of animals. The flowers are pollinated by bees, the soil is aerated by worms, the ground is fertilised by herds of animals and even in the day of the internal combustion engine there are still vehicles or ploughs pulled by animals that are stronger than ourselves. The human responsibility to till the earth and look after it has had the vast majority of its work done by animals. We may be the managers but we would be lost without these, our partners.

If we wonder why some of the angelic beings in the Bible have the appearance of animals (eg, the living creatures of Ezek. 1:4-14 and Rev. 4:6-8), one answer may be that as animals are to us – helpers – so are the angels to God.

So, will there be animals in the new heaven and the new earth? *Can I expect to see my pet in the next life?* To ask such questions is to be setting too small an agenda, to be bringing God's wonderful future down to the level of our present familiar life. In effect we are saying, 'I want to carry on just as before.'

The next life will be so overwhelmingly wonderful (1 Cor. 2:9), that such issues will fade from view. Certainly we would expect our future existence to be superior to the present in every way, so animals might indeed be included (Isa. 11:6-9). But these are no more than hints, for the Bible is a book that talks primarily to the *human* situation.

Q.11

Who or what are angels?

My 'New Age' friends talk a lot about angels. What are they?

There is plenty to learn. The Bible has far more to tell us about angels than 'New Age' gurus ever could!

1. Angels are worshippers around God's throne

They belong to an heavenly order of spiritual, created beings but they are not like God and therefore not to be worshipped. Essentially, they serve God in worship and praise. At the limited times when they have become visible (as in special visitations, or in prophetic visions) they reflect the awesome holiness and harmony of heaven (Dan. 7:9,10; Rev. 5:11,12).

2. Angels carry out God's will

They are numerous and may be known by different terms (*holy ones, messengers, sons of God*). The 'cherubim' (plural of 'cherub') are presented in Scripture as winged creatures, flying to fulfil God's commands, guarding the way to his presence and acting as carriers of God on his throne (Ps. 89:5; Gen. 3:24; Exo. 25:18-22; Ezek. 1:4-24).

3. Angels are witnesses to God's saving acts

They are present around the time of Jesus' birth, death, resurrection and ascension. They will also announce his final return. They are said by Jesus to rejoice at the repentance of a sinner, and he says they will be involved in the collecting together of his redeemed people (Luke 2:8-15; 22:43; 24:4-8; Acts 1:10,11; 1 Thess. 4:16; Luke 15:10; Matt. 24:30,31).

4. Angels are messengers at times of revelation

Angels have acted as announcers at the beginning of God's great eras – at the commissioning of prophets, at the start of the Gospel story and when

Gentiles were welcomed into the church. These announcements were received with a variety of reactions – with awe, fear, astonishment and joy (Isa. 6:1-7; Luke 1:26-33; Acts 10:1-8).

5. Angels are fighters at times of conflict

The Bible teaches of an angelic rebellion and fall under Satan, 'the serpent', 'the Devil', 'the father of lies' and 'Accuser'. Although his defeat was assured by the victory of Christ's death, evil itself will not be finally banished until his destruction (Luke 10:18; 2 Kings 6:17; Dan. 12:1; Rev. 12:7-9).

6. Angels are ministers at times of crisis

In many places in the Bible, patriarchs, prophets, apostles, and indeed Jesus himself, received ministry and help from angels at particular moments of stress, temptation or danger.

All Christians may receive their protection and support. Whilst we may be thankful to them, they are not to be worshipped as go-betweens between us and God – only Christ has that place. We are also not to place too much emphasis on them as it can lead to distortions of the faith (Gen. 19:15; 1 Kings 19:5-7; Matt. 4:11; Acts. 12:7-10; Heb. 1:14; Col. 2:18).

PS: Old Testament accounts of 'the' Angel of the Lord (see ch. 29) refer to the Second Person of the Trinity, Christ – the 'Sent One' – as he existed before he came to earth (eg, Genesis 16:7; 22:11; Exodus 3:2).

FOR FURTHER STUDY: *Open Home, Open Bible* video/DVD series, cassette 6, programme 1. Enquiries: vestry@allsouls.org (for USA, www.visionvideo.com).

Q.12

How big was the flood?

A Mesopotamian disaster, or a world catastrophe? The Flood continues to create discussion.

We don't even have to explain which flood we're talking about; Noah's Flood is firmly embedded in the human memory on every continent.

There is a *Hindu tradition* about a great flood, and a ship of safety finally landing on a northern mountain. *In China*, Fa-he, the founder of Chinese civilisation, is represented as escaping from the waters of a flood and reappears as the first man in a new world, accompanied by his wife, three sons and three daughters; eight people in all. There is the famous *Babylonian Epic of Gilgamesh* with its detailed myth-legend of a great flood. *The Fiji islanders* have accounts of a flood in which a family of eight was saved. In *South America*, paintings have been discovered, representing a flood, a man and his wife on a raft, with a mountain featuring in the story, as well as a dove. The *Cherokee Indians* have a similar story. Only Africa seems to be without a traditional flood story.

Christians and Jews say that the book of Genesis gives us the original, inspired and accurate account of this mega event. The legends in other countries could have come from Shem, one of Noah's sons, who later told his children of this great epic of his life. As the human race fanned outwards from Mesopotamia so the story travelled outwards as well – becoming garbled in the process, and mixed up with legend and folk-lore.

How big was the Flood, then? The right answer is that it was of all-time, universal dimension and significance. We can make out a strong case for a literal world-wide flood – with the release of the great waters from both below and above (Gen. 7:11,12). However, we can also note that the phrase of Genesis 7:19 – that *'all the high mountains under the entire heavens were covered'* can be paralleled by Acts 2:5, where – on the Day of Pentecost – those who were present were *'from every nation under heaven'*. Those nations are then listed out in detail, and they are not from all the countries in the world but from around the Mediterranean basin – the then known world of Luke the writer. So the Flood itself *need* not have extended across the entire world.

Can we respect the differing views among reverent students of Scripture? If we cannot, we are in deep trouble. Once we get into lengthy and heated debates as to whether the flood covered every dot of land-space on the world, we are in serious danger of exhausting ourselves and diverting people from hearing the *real* message of the Flood. What is it?

First, it shows the problem humans were in, it takes the story of the Bible from a garden to the whole world! The Flood conveys a universal warning.

Second, it produces a model for our entire understanding of judgment and grace. Ultimately, the safety of the ark, for those who went in, is a parallel with the spiritual safety offered by Christ – for those who believe.

Third, it sets the stage for the drama of salvation that unfolds from Genesis 12 onwards.

Q.13

In touch – through Yoga?

How far does Yoga provide a valid way to meditate and be at peace with the world and the universe?

The word *Yoga* means 'union', and in Hindu philosophy the person who practises it does so to be better at self-control and, more importantly, to reach union with the 'Infinite' – who/which can be described in lots of different ways.

So, even though someone new to a Yoga class may be reassured that the exercises are 'non-religious', it still represents a Hindu world-view. 'Yoga', says one of its top advocates, 'is not a Friday night or Sunday morning practice; it is an entire way of life and should occupy 24 hours of every day'. The little 'popular' books on Yoga never tell you that! In Yoga we are presented with:

1. An alternative interpretation of the universe

'Position One', in a standard book, begins with: 'Mantra: Om adi deva nameh. Here we face the spiritual son. Standing upright with the breath suspended, fully composed, we represent Purusha, the primeval god Adi Deva, at the very beginning of time'.

The basic Yoga 'Lotus position', in which a circle is made of thumb and forefinger – implies the unbrokenness of life in a never-ending circle of successive reincarnations. But that is not how the Christian sees life on this world (Heb. 9:27). Just to read Colossians chapter 2 gives us the Christian viewpoint. How then does Yoga view God?

2. A degraded image of God

Another quote: 'This posture, Hanum-an-asana... *Hanuman* was the name of a powerful monkey chief who was the son of Anjana and the devoted friend and servant of Rama, the seventh incarnation of Vishnu....'

A contrast with Colossians 2:6-10 shows the main difference between the main Hindu concept behind Yoga and the revealed truth of God in Jesus Christ. To go down the Yoga route is to shift towards a *pantheistic* standpoint. One in which God is identified with nature, and finally towards a *monistic* view, where God is thought of as an impersonal 'It', without form or personality.

3. A negative view of who you are
Another quote: 'You will literally be moving, being in the nothing. The experience of nothing is Yoga'.

But the art of emptying one's mind is foreign to the Christian – who doesn't focus on nothing, nor even upon ourselves, but upon Christ (Col. 3:1,2). Paradoxically, in finding Christ we discover ourselves and our identity becomes enhanced with the fullness of life that he promises (Col. 2:10).

4. A wrong view of being saved from sin
The 'sin' question is never raised in Yoga, and the answer to sin – the Cross of Christ – is never in view. Yoga offers only 'enlightenment' for the ignorant. **It has no answer to the problem of the wrong things we do and our meeting with a holy and just God.**

Breathing exercises and meditation (upon Christ and his Word) are commendable. But we are unwise to open the door for the entry of a system that, in Paul's words, causes someone to lose connection with our head, Christ himself (Col. 2:19).

Q.14

Back into the past?

What is the Christian to make of claims to people remembering a previous life, or of events that took place even centuries earlier?

The subject of retro-cognition [seeing into the past] is a very fascinating one, and a good deal has been written about it.

One of the most famous instances involved two women (both of high intelligence) who claimed, when walking in the Garden of Versailles in France, to have stepped back from 1901 to 1789. They 'saw' paths, buildings and even fashions that precisely corresponded to those of an earlier age. Naturally stories like this are open to challenge. Perhaps the Christian makes several thoughtful observations.

1. We are children of our own time

That is, our lives are set within a time process. They are given to us as a one-off, never-to-be-repeated, challenge. 'Only one life is allotted us', wrote Alexander Solzhenitsyn, 'one small, short life!' And we are told to make the most of the present opportunity (Eph. 5:16).

Other eras have their fascination for us, and we can learn from them, but we are only in the present for a short time and the potential of the present can easily be weakened by time-consuming speculation. However:

2. We are children of eternity

God 'has put eternity into man's mind' (Eccles. 3:11). God, in whose image we are made, is not bound by time so it is not too much of a stretch to think that sometimes individuals could have received a reminder – if no more than a whisper in a dream – of the divine and eternal context of their creation; receiving flashes of insight into things that have happened (or may yet happen) outside of our present time. The secular humanist, who only believes in what they can sense physically, will never be able to understand this but we do, knowing that we are 'fearfully and wonderfully made' (Ps. 139:14).

3. We are children who are responsible for our actions

The second half of Ecclesiastes 3:11 tells us that God has limited us so that we cannot find out what he has done from the beginning to the end. We are not know-alls. What we do know gives us a moral responsibility as to what to do with that knowledge.

Deuteronomy 29:29 expresses it perfectly: 'The secret things belong to the Lord our God, but the things revealed belong to us and to our children for ever, *that we may follow all the words of this law.*' God has revealed some of his secrets to prophets. They used this perception, to point people to the Lord; something quite different from the activity of the clairvoyant or fortune-teller, who has no brief to point people to scripture truth.

If there *is* a biblical retro-cognition then it will be the one in operation at the final Judgment. When 'the books are opened' and men and women will be able to look back upon their past life – *this life.* There is no reincarnation, no other life that should occupy our attention, because it is appointed to us **once** to die, and after that, the judgment (Heb. 9:27).

Q.15

Did the sun stop still?

Can you help me over Joshua 10:12–14, about the sun standing still during Joshua's battle? I guess God *could* stop the world moving round if he wanted to. But did he?

It's important that we rely on the Bible text itself, rather than rush off to consult the scientists or archaeologists! The answer will be right here. Significantly, in other scripture passages relating to this event, there is no reference to an astronomical act of God, either in Isaiah 28:21 – where the victory at Gibeon is quoted – or in the exploits of faith in Hebrews 11. There is a possible hint at what is happening only in Habakkuk 3:11.

Sure, the elements were on Joshua's side! It reminds us of Judges 5:20: *The stars in their courses fought against Sisera.* The quote referred to here is from the 'lost' book of Jasher, celebrating Israel's heroes: *O sun, stand still over Gibeon, O moon, over the Valley of Aijalon.*

Question: Was Joshua wishing for more daylight, in order to make certain of victory? If so, it is like the classical story of Agamemnon, who prays that the sun may not go down till he has sacked Troy. **Or was Joshua, in fact, wishing for a little more *darkness*?** 'What!' you may say? And at first the comment of verse 13 doesn't read like that. 'The sun stopped in the middle of the sky and delayed going down about a full day.'

But as you look at the earlier report of the battle, there is evidence here to think again about the meaning. The battle's crisis point coincided with a devastating hailstorm (v.11). We also learn that the battle began just after an all-night march, so it was the *dawn* that was advancing too quickly for Joshua's liking!

But that still leaves us with 13? Surely it means that more daylight is required? Hebrew scholars say that the word for *stand still* can equally well mean 'cease'; for example in 2 Kings 4:6, 'Then the oil stopped flowing' or 'ceased'.

As for the idea of the sun 'going down', it was Professor F.F. Bruce who observed that while the Hebrew word *bo* usually applies to sunset, there is an instance, in a poetic setting, where *bo* ('to come') is parallel to *zarah* **'to rise'**, as in Isaiah 60:1: 'Arise, shine...' (compare Job 31:26). So it is not only possible, but likely, that after the night march, Joshua needed extra hours of darkness to complete his night exercise, and that this was given by means of the massive hailstorm that blotted out everything – sun, moon, the lot.

Is this too far-fetched? Twisting words – in order to avoid some scientific embarrassment! No, this is Bible study. Even the mention, in verse 12, of the geographical position of the sun over Gibeon (in the east) and the moon over Aijalon (in the west) is a firm indication that Joshua's prayer that both sun and moon would 'cease' was uttered in the early morning.

Both sun and moon died on them that day and never put in an appearance at all. It was a miraculous answer to prayer.

Q.16

What is the origin of evil spirits?

Where do evil spirits come from, and how are we to view the unseen world of evil and occultism?

Evil spirits come from the ranks of created angels (ch. 6). They were not *created* as evil beings, for all of God's creation was good (Gen. 3:1). The Bible indicates that a number of angels, headed by Satan, or Lucifer, rebelled against God's authority (Isa. 14:12-15; Ezek. 28:11-19).

The Serpent, Satan, is leader of the fallen angels and opposes himself to God. But evil and good are not co-equal. *Dualism* (belief in the equal and permanent existence of evil alongside the good) has no place in the Bible. The translation 'crafty' as applied to Satan (Gen. 3:1 NIV and ESV) is unhelpful here. It suggests that the serpent was *created* evil. The King James Version 'subtle' (or 'clever', 'talented') is correct. Unlike goodness, evil has a beginning and an end. The end will come because Satan's final destruction is already assured (Rev. 12:12; 20:10).

The world of the occult (from the Latin: *occultus*, 'secret', 'hidden'), is the intrusion into the forbidden territory of **superstition, fortune telling, magic** and **spiritism** (see ch. 69). Its downfall is finally assured through Jesus. His early ministry established a bridgehead against the evil unseen world; so the demons reacted in hostile, and sometimes violent, ways (Mark 1:23-27; 32-34).

Jesus had no fear of demons, and neither should we if we are Christians. It is important that Christians avoid becoming obsessed by the unseen world to the extent that we become either intimidated or fascinated. I remember in London, after the showing of a film that featured the occult, that about twenty cinema viewers went for counselling under the impression that they had been 'taken over' by evil spirits. They had not. All recovered after a course of prescribed tablets. They had only been victims of suggestion.

We are wise, then, not to imagine that every sin, habit, illness or misfortune is due directly to the activity of the Devil and must therefore be 'exorcised'. Terrible damage has been done in this respect by well-meaning, but uninformed Christian leaders.

Faced by Christ's authority the kingdom of spirits has no option but to shrink and retreat. Magic spells and charms have no power over the true Christian (provided we do not open ourselves to their influence) for 'the one who is in you is greater than the one who is in the world' (1 John 4:4). If we resist the devil, he will flee from us (James 4:7). All occultism is to be ruthlessly left out of our lives (eg, Lev. 19:31; 20:6; 1 Sam. 28 – with 1 Chron. 10:13; Isa. 8:19,20; Acts 19:18-20).

The demonic world is already doomed and defeated (Col. 2:15; Heb. 2:14,15). **It is the death of Jesus that has achieved this victory.** We are to be confident, but not laid back. Although the victory is guaranteed, Satan's kingdom has yet to concede its defeat at the Cross. Its final destruction will be at the return of Christ.

Q.17

What are territorial spirits?

Is it possible that a powerful evil spirit can occupy a neighbourhood, city or country but through prayer and spiritual warfare we can assist the angels to win?

The growth of the idea of 'territorial spirits' became highlighted around the mid-1980s, partly through a number of popular writers.

The teaching is based on the belief that Satan has assigned a core of demons to different geographical and political areas of the world. The only way to defeat them, we are told, is through the prayers and fasting of Christian believers. This will enable us to receive a given 'word' of knowledge from God about those behind the demonic activity, so that we can confront it and destroy it.

First of all, we must recognise that we can easily underestimate, or ignore, the works of the devil and his angels. We must always be alert to this (Eph. 6:10-20).

Is the idea of territorial spirits biblical? The teaching certainly *appeals* to Scripture, notably Daniel 10, with its reference to the 'Prince' of Persia and Greece; also Acts 13, where Paul in Cyprus, confronts Elymas the sorcerer; and Matthew 12:29, with its words about *binding*, or tying up, the intruding 'strong man'. The deduction is made that if a demon can inhabit a house, it can inhabit a tribe or a city.

Here we must question the logic. The argument is heavily based upon *experience*. For example, it was claimed that an African tribe only became 'open' to the Gospel when some of its members were taken to another area where the demonic hold was less strong. Similarly, missionaries, suffering from illnesses and satanic pressure opposing them, would only recover – it was claimed – when flown out of the region. Here are some critical points that need to be made:

1. Don't give too great an attention to formulas when the Bible doesn't give them. Certainly for many years the Masai people of East Africa seemed impenetrable to the Gospel. But the eventual break-through came not by moving them somewhere else but by sustained intercessory prayer over a considerable period. Thousands of Masai became Christians right there in their *own* 'territory'.

2. Do pay attention to the full message of the Bible. The Bible is all we need. **If you concentrate on a few selected passages then you risk going wrong.** For example, the Bible says that the forces against the Christian are *the world, the flesh and the devil.* By adopting the above ideas we lump problems with the first two categories into the third – that of the devil alone. One possible outcome of dualistic teaching (see ch. 16) is that Christians can develop an obsession with the Devil and his power that is bigger than it is.

3. Putting attention in the wrong place means that we ignore the real weapons of our faith – the preaching of the Cross. When the New Testament apostles were faced with the entire, heathen, continent of Europe, they didn't require a special word of knowledge or superior wisdom. *They already knew what they had to do.* Look up 1 Corinthians 2:1-5, and you'll see.

Q.18

Were the Magi astrologers?

Over this past Christmas I've heard that the wise men, who came to see the infant Jesus, were astrologers. But isn't astrology something to do with the occult?

It shows that you are thinking things through that you ask this question. The Scriptures are consistently hostile to all occult activity (Isa. 8:19).

However, we may (in fact we must!) investigate things that God has chosen to *reveal* to us in the Bible, and not least when it involves prophecy, like this passage does.

The birth of Jesus, and the star that told us of his birth, was the activity of God himself. *This was nothing to do with horoscopes.* At significant stages of Jesus' life, supernatural things happened: the dove at his baptism; the light at his transfiguration; the darkness and earthquake at his death; the cloud at his ascension. These showed whom Jesus was to those who had minds to understand tham. In a similar way then, at his birth, there was a star.

The significance of the wise men, or the 'Magi' as they have been termed, is that they were Gentiles, probably from Mesopotamia. They would not have benefited directly from the privileges of Judaism or its Scriptures. However, it is very likely that they would have taken note of a prophecy that had been uttered centuries earlier by a Gentile prophet whose name was Balaam.

In fact, he was even from their own area, a place called Pethor by the river Euphrates (Num. 22:4,5). His words would have been remembered down the ages:

> I see him, but not now; I behold him, but not near.
> A star will come out of Jacob; a sceptre will rise out of Israel (Num. 24:17).

The star stood for royal power and splendour so the second line is a firm indication of kingship. Further lines of the prophecy point to the widespread rule of this coming King. When a special star came to the attention of the Magi, they had to investigate further.

1. Their sensitivity to revelation

Traditionally it seems that the Magi (who were a kind of priestly tribe) were to the Persians what the Levites were to Israel; they were respected instructors to the Persian kings. Their questioning minds caused them to recognise, and then follow, the star when it appeared.

2. Their persistence in the search

On reaching Jerusalem, the Magi caused great disruption by asking where the new king had been born. Herod's advisors looked up the prophecies, and announced Bethlehem as the location (Micah 5:2). *But none of Herod's advisors made the journey to Bethlehem* – it was left to these Gentile teachers to go and pay their respects to Israel's king.

3. Their reverence for the infant

Worship – not power – was their aim. These were not occult princes seeking to use their secret (occult) knowledge to gain power. They were totally unlike Simon Magus (Acts 8:9-11); who through his exploits wanted to be 'great'. That is how occultism works: using secret knowledge to promote yourself. Not so, the Magi of Matthew 2. They were wise with the wisdom that seeks God, and were obedient to him.

Q.19

Why doesn't God intervene?

As I look at the violence and persecution of the world today, at the racial and religious strife, I long for God to intervene. Surely he could put these things right at a single stroke?

Christians, of all people, should be encouraged because – as Chapter 6 suggests – God's promise to deal with evil follows hard on the heels of the sin of Adam and Eve (Gen. 3:15). One day there will be a child born who will crush the serpent's head.

'But why not now?' we ask. The answer is that for God in Christ to right all the wrongs of the human race at a single stroke would mean wiping out the *human race* at a single stroke. Many people long that violence and pain could be banished but the answer to our question is itself a question: '**How righteous are YOU?** What is the risk of *you* being wiped out with the rest of the evil-doers if God was going to end the troubles just like that? (Pretty high, I guess!)'

The Bible teaches that God *is* going to act at a single stroke. In fact it keeps warning us that he will (Zeph. 1:2,18; Rev. 20:10,14). But when it happens, it will be on a day, and at a time, known only to him (Matt. 24:36). And it will be the end of this world.

Until that time comes we are presented in the Scriptures with a God of amazing patience, 'not wanting anyone to perish, but everyone to come to repentance' (2 Peter 3:9). So we do not have action at a single stroke because if it were to happen everyone would go down under the judgment required to set the balances right.

So God waits; he works; he agonises; he grieves; he sends messenger after messenger – prophet after prophet; doctors and aid agencies too. *He's not required to* but out of love, he keeps going. Many of those he sends are rejected. It is a pattern of his mission (Heb. 11:32-38). Finally the Lord comes himself in the person of Jesus: still working, loving, wooing. He suffers hell's agonies, himself, on the Cross.

It is there that we see that God is the greatest sufferer in the universe.

The Bible teaches us that God has acted, once and for all, in Jesus Christ to deal with our greatest problem – unforgiven sin. On coming to Christ and his Cross, men and women are forgiven, even of the most hideous sins, for he has endured God's judgement on even the worst sins in our place. There is only one qualification – that we repent and believe. There are many who refuse his offer.

We are still being given time – that is the situation – and while believers can never afford to be complacent we can certainly be confident because we know the end result. It is going to happen, as prophesied. If you have a clear view of the future then the present makes sense. It is only if we have an fuzzy view of the future that our lives will seem meaningless.

Q.20

Will the universe implode?

I have read that the universe was about the size of a table-tennis ball when it began and that it will eventually return to the same size at the end of its life. Will it?

Too often Christians are overcritical of the theories of scientists; we should encourage people to be like Sir Isaac Newton who exercised what he called 'the power of patient thought' in the unravelling of the universe's secrets. But remember, *theories* are just that, they keep changing.

It is likely that no one will get the end entirely right! Even those of us who read the Scriptures will be dumbfounded at the finish. None of us will nod sagely and say *'Huh! Exactly as I'd predicted'*. In our fallenness we can't see as clearly as we think and can all too easily get it wrong, despite the clear signposts God gives us! Few were ready for the birth at Bethlehem; the disciples were demoralised at the death of Jesus (despite him telling them it was going to happen!); the resurrection, when it happened, was a bombshell among them; the Ascension caught them totally off guard, gazing upwards in mystification; the Gift of the Spirit, though predicted, was an amazing surprise.

So when the sixth saving act of Christ – his return at the final triumph – takes place, once again we shall gasp, 'I never thought it would be like that!'

We are told that we shall survive the ending of this world. There will be no table-tennis balls but rather *the bending round of the two covers of the Bible to meet each other*. Moses, who wrote the first five books of the Bible, will shake hands with John, the writer of the Revelation. The story will be complete. It will be the same heaven and earth, recognisably so, but completely overhauled. The tie-up between Genesis and Revelation – with some 1,600 years separating their writing – is inspired and brilliant.

Genesis records how God created the heavens and the earth; Revelation tells us about the *new* heavens and the *new* earth. In Genesis the various lights of nature are created; the sun, moon and stars; Revelation tells us that in the new order the only light that we will need will be provided by the glory of God and of the Lamb – Christ.

Genesis at the beginning describes a garden that was lost; the final book of the Bible reveals a restored garden *city*. Genesis speaks of a lying serpent; Revelation tells of the devil being thrown into a lake of burning sulphur. In Genesis, the man and woman are running from God; in Revelation 21 the ban is lifted and God lives freely with his people again.

Genesis shows us the tree of life, denied to Adam and Eve by an angel with a flaming sword. In Revelation, those who have their 'robes washed' at the Cross of Christ now *have the right to the tree of life* and have access to the gates of the city.

We're seeing the video run-down of history in advance. I feel a bit like a TV sports announcer saying '**If you don't want to know the final result, then turn your eyes away (from the last pages of the Bible) now!**

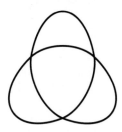

PART TWO
THE TRUTH WE BELIEVE

Then said the Proconsul, 'I have wild beasts; if thou repent not I will throw thee to them.' But he said, 'Send for them. For repentance from better to worse is not a change permitted to us; but to change from cruelty to righteousness is a noble thing.'

Then said the Pronconsul again, 'If thou dost despise the wild beasts I will make thee to be consumed by fire, if thou repent not.'

And Polycarp answered, 'Thou threatenest the fire that burns for an hour and in a little while is quenched; for thou knowest not of the fire of the judgment to come, and the fire of the eternal punishment, reserved for the ungodly. But why delayest thou? Bring what thou wilt.'

Bishop of Smyrna,
The Martyrdom of Polycarp, AD155

Q.21

Has anything changed in 2,000 years?

Why is it that after 2,000 years Christianity seems so powerless to change society?

Let's get it clear, it's not Christianity but *Christ* who has power to change anything and anybody! Those early apostles believed that the multi-cultural world-view that faced them in Europe would give way as they preached Jesus Christ.... *and it did.*

Faced by the Gospel the opponents of the early church failed on four fronts – they couldn't…

   – produce a satisfying *understanding* of what life was about.
   – come up with a believable *morality* (their Gods were totally *immoral*).
   – testify to a personal *faith* (instead they had superstitious fear).
   – find an answer to *death.*

On all four counts the new Christian preachers had answers that glowed with transforming power.

   These followers of Jesus **'out-lived'** their neighbours, not in how many years they lived but in the way they lived. Hermas, a former slave of the period wrote, 'The Holy Spirit was a *glad* spirit'. But they also **'out-died'** their contemporaries, countless thousands of them being killed in ten mighty persecutions that took place in the first three hundred years after Christ. Their faith *'was worth martyrdom'*, as one historian observed. Further, they also **'out-thought'** their critics; asking awkward questions about the superstitions of their day and getting rid of demons through calling on Christ's powerful name. Steadily, across Europe, a new world-view replaced the old. Even the Parthenon, Athens' great temple of paganism, became a Christian church and remained so for a thousand years.

Yet, Christ's humble followers have only very rarely occupied the seats of worldly power. *The reason is that Christ's kingdom is not of this world* (John 18:36). It has no armies, navies or banks. It raises no taxes. It holds no elections. It seeks no government posts. But, wherever its representatives are faithful to the Scripture and live out its message, human experience agrees with the statement of the historian T.R. Glover, *The Christian religion stabilises society without sterilising it.*

Go to any country of the world where Christian preaching is outlawed, where the Bible is banned and where another religion is enforced on pain of death and see the difference in society! Countless citizens escape to other countries, anxious to escape the restricted wasteland created by such 'sterility'. Where do they flee to? Usually to a country where the Gospel has at some time been freely preached, and where the beneficial effects still show.

And that brings me to my last point. *Every new generation has to rise to the challenge of the Gospel.* The evangelists John and Charles Wesley, at a time of spiritual and moral decline, resolved that they were going to change the course of history – and they did. But you and I can't rest on their achievements. **It is up to us to prove the power of Christ for ourselves once again – today. Has he changed you?**

Q.22

How can I explain the Trinity to people of other religions?

As a student, I get so frustrated when talking with non-Christian groups at my campus about the Trinity.

I salute you for the attempt! Don't bother with philosophical arguments, illustrations or stories; they don't help (Isaiah 40:18).

The Bible is your authority. Remember that to most religions Jesus didn't arrive until the middle of their history! But if Christ is not present *from the beginning*, then he can hardly be a universal world Saviour. So start with the Old Testament and present the one living, Trinitarian God who is seen as three persons *throughout the Bible*. Jesus has been there since the beginning, Genesis 1:1 has *Elohim* for 'God', a plural noun, but with a singular verb. 'Let **us** make man in **our** image' (Gen. 1:26). So at the beginning God is described as more than 'one'.

Focus on Exodus 33. This is the advice of theologian, Paul Blackham. Tell your friends the story of Exodus, and of the 'Angel of the Lord' (who, by the way, is the Christ, before he became a man – see chapter 23), who accompanies his people in the pillars of cloud and fire to Mount Sinai. Moses is called up the mountain to meet with 'the Lord', but he is also said regularly to meet in a tent at the foot of the mountain with someone also called 'the Lord', who speaks to him **'face to face, as a man speaks to his friend'** (Exodus 33:11). Yet when Moses is up the mountain, and asks the Lord to show himself, he is told, **'You cannot see my face, for no one may see me and live'** (Exodus 33:20).

There is no contradiction. Moses has no problem with the God who is *one*, and yet who is presented as these **two** Persons. In addition, *the Holy Spirit*, only two chapters on is said to help God's people and is also called 'the Lord' (Exod. 35:30,31; compare chapter 36:1). Other helpful references are

Nehemiah 9:20 and Isaiah 63:9-14. So we have **three** persons – all called 'the Lord' – or God.

It is a pattern throughout Scripture; there is **the Father** who we don't see – who lives in the heavens above his people; there is **the Son** who has been seen – and who makes him known (John 1:18) and comes among his people; there is **the Spirit**, who is unseen, yet lives within and helps his people. *The Trinity is basic to our salvation* – for these three Persons, in the one Godhead, have combined to save us from our sins. All three work together; In the **will** of the Father, the saving **work** of the Son, and the **witness** of the Holy Spirit living within us (John 14:16, 23-26; Rom. 8:16,17). Try that as a start with your friends.

FURTHER STUDY: This material can be filled out further by Dr Paul Blackham's excellent audio cassette (WS5) on 'Explaining the Trinity', from Billy Graham's Amsterdam 2000, P.O. Box 1270, Charlotte, NC, 28201-1270, USA. Also obtainable through the All Souls Tape Library at Langham Place, London, vestry@allsouls.org). Also try *Shared Life*, Donald Macleod, Christian Focus Publications.

Q.23

The invisible God appearing?

Is my teacher right in saying that when God is said to 'speak' or 'appear' to people (eg, Gen. 17:1), it is just "naïve people making God up to be like themselves"?

Not at all. Very simply, the 'appearings' of the Lord God in the Old Testament are pointing to the coming into this world of the second person of the Trinity [the pre-incarnate Christ]. When John writes that Isaiah *saw Jesus' glory* (John 12:41) he is quoting Isaiah chapter 6, where the prophet had shouted out in terror, 'My eyes have **seen** the King, the Lord Almighty'. *It was Christ that Isaiah saw.*

How does that square with 'No one has ever seen God at any time' (John 1:18)? Invariably in the Old Testament, when God *does* appear, and speak with people, it is the pre-incarnate Christ who does so. Nebuchadnezzar sees the three intended victims he has thrown into the burning furnace joined by a fourth person (Dan. 3:25); of course, it was Christ.

The Son has these different titles in the Old Testament. Sometimes he is simply the **Lord God** – walking in the cool of the day; making garments of skin for Adam and Eve (Gen. 3:8,21) or shutting the door of the ark (Gen. 7:16); he is seen by Daniel as the **Son of Man**, a divine being (Dan. 7:13); but he is also **the Word of the Lord**, someone who speaks, for example, to Abraham (Gen. 15:1-6). When we read that Abraham 'believed the Lord', it was Christ he was believing.

Whenever we read of the Lord 'appearing' to Abraham and 'speaking' to him (Gen. 17:1; 18:1), it is not someone making up a God that is like us and so can speak to us. We are actually reading about Christ. When Jacob wrestles with God in the form of 'a man', he calls the place 'Peniel' (*face of God*), 'because I saw God face to face, and yet my life was spared' (Gen. 32:30). Who was that God, a God who was a man? We know all too well.

In the Old Testament, the Lord God whom people see is frequently referred to as the **Angel of the Lord** (as distinct from 'angels' or 'an angel') – it means *Sent One*. For example, 'the angel of the Lord' says, 'I brought you up out of Egypt and led you into the land that I swore to give to your forefathers. I said, "I will never break my covenant with you..." (Judg. 2:1-4). There are similar references in Genesis 16:7,11,13 and Judges 13:21,22.

At the burning bush Moses meets 'the angel of the Lord', who defines himself as the God of Abraham, Isaac and Jacob (Exod. 3:2,6). This is Christ who in the New Testament referred to himself many times as '**the one sent** from the Father' (John 6:38). It is this same angel of the Lord who travels with his people in a visible pillar of cloud and fire (Exod. 14:19,20).

It is a consistent picture throughout. It matches the New Testament declaration that Christ 'is the image (Greek: the *ikon*) of the invisible God' (Col. 1:15). I wonder if that might help your teacher?

Q.24

Where does Jesus fit in?

God I understand, but I can't see where Jesus fits into the picture.

A theologian called Athanasius, Egyptian by birth and Greek by education, gave the answer to your question sixteen hundred years ago. He said, *the only system of thought into which Jesus Christ will **fit** is the one in which **he** is the starting point!*

If we try to begin to understand God, and the meaning of life, from a purely human viewpoint – let alone the place that Christ has in the universe – we'll be like the man who tries to do up his shirt buttons *beginning with the wrong button.* He may hope that it will all work out, and that the shirt will eventually fit properly.... but it never will.

So don't begin with your understanding – begin with *Christ* – if you want the picture to make sense. He is right there from the start (chs. 22 and 23). All creation starts and finishes with him. He called himself the alpha and Omega (the first and last letters in the Greek alphabet – another way of saying the beginning and the end). He is its rightful heir (Col. 1:15-17). You will notice from Colossians 1:17 that, it is not Christ who fits into *our* system but that we can only 'fit' – finding balance and meaning – in *his* (or rather, in HIM).

It is through Christ alone that we can know the face of God, and his salvation in our lives. He is both fully God *and* fully human. Christ, *the God-Man,* is the perfect mediator because he sees both sides. When he died, he bridged the gulf between heaven and earth (Phil. 2:5-11).

No one else will do. That was the blazing conviction of those first-century Christians. Beside Christ there was *no other name* (Acts 4:12) – or to put it another way *no one who was capable of bringing God and man together.* Historically Christ's name claims to be greater in all the areas of life that matter most. It happened **in the world of worship** – where the Druids, ju-ju men, witch doctors, temple priests and the gigantic gods Mithras, Serapis, Jupiter and Venus were all swept away.

It also happened **in the world of suffering.** When we put the greatest leaders and thinkers of history together it is quite clear that none of them suffered as Jesus did. In him we see God incarnate, living among us, loving, suffering, dying and reclaiming us for his kingdom. This fact alone is enough to explain the beginning of hospitals in our world – *they were never begun by a State department.* Our compassion is a reflection of part of God's character.

It happened **in the world of creativity.** Christ has inspired symphonies, paintings, soaring architecture and great literature. These reflect God's creative nature in our character. Take Christ away, and the writings of Shakespeare would be meaningless. Atheism, by its very nature could never have this impact, for atheism has no wings, it only knows *what it is not.*

It happened **in the world of eternity.** One pre-Christian epitaph says '*I was not, I was born, I lived, I am not, that is all*'. Xenophanes wrote '*Guesswork is over all*'. Into that world exploded the message of Christ, physically raised from death, never to die again. That message alone is enough to change our view of the entire universe – and the universe itself only works because of Christ.

Q.25

Should we pray to Mary?

Is it valid to address – and pray to – Mary, as the Mother of God?

It is probably not surprising that the respect in which Mary, the mother of Jesus, has always been held, has led some people to move to revere her, and from reverence to even move to prayer and worship.

But the Gospel writers are very careful about Mary. They were very restrained with their references to her. Is she someone who people can turn to in prayer in the hope that she can put in a word on their behalf to Christ. A go-between, or mediator, between us and him? Let me suggest three reasons that should discourage us from doing so:

1. Praying to Mary contradicts the example of the apostles

The New Testament contains many of the prayers of God's inspired leaders. In none of them does anyone pray to Mary. The apostle Paul prays like this for his friends at Ephesus, that the Father 'may strengthen you with power through his Spirit in your inner being, so that Christ may dwell in your hearts through faith' (Eph. 3:14-21). All three Persons of the Trinity are in that prayer – and the fact that Mary is not mentioned is consistent with the whole New Testament witness.

2. Praying to Mary contradicts the attitude of Mary herself

Why was Mary selected to be the mother of Jesus? We can readily point to her modesty, her sense of dependence upon the Lord and her obedience. On one of the few occasions that her words are recorded, she referred to herself as God's *handmaiden*, or 'servant'. Far from associating herself with God's saving actions, Mary identifies herself instead with the rest of needy humanity in her words, '...and my spirit rejoices in God *my Saviour*' (Luke 1:47).

Although 'highly favoured' and destined to be called 'blessed' by future generations (Luke 1:28,48), what we know of Mary's character indicates that she would have hated an extravagant title like 'Mother of God', or any description of her beyond those given to her in the Scriptures.

3. Praying to Mary undermines the truth of the Incarnation

The whole point of God taking our form as a human being and living among us was that in Jesus Christ we were given a real flesh and blood go-between with God. *None other is needed.* Christ is someone we can go to directly, in the knowledge that through Him we have a hearing at the very throne of God (Heb. 7:25). We can get in immediately through Christ, the one and only mediator that we could ever need (1 Tim. 2:5).

We can agree with Article 22 of the Church of England, where prayers to the saints are rejected as something that is '*grounded upon no warranty of Scripture*'.

Q.26.

Is faith a leap in the dark?

I know older people who said that they became Christians when they were my age but now say they have grown out of their faith. Can you explain how one could ever be a believer without committing intellectual suicide?

Certainly the problem with some Christians is that, while they grow bigger physically and get educated, they never grow up spiritually. They pray the same childhood prayers, they by-pass everyday moral and social issues – they've never left the Sunday School. You obviously don't wish that.

There are three stages that a believer must go through, if faith is to be real. The first is **credulity**; when we accept what our elders teach us because we trust them. The second is **criticism**; when we flex our muscles and start to examine our beliefs – even to the point of leaving them behind because they have not become our own. The third, and vital, stage we must arrive at is **conviction**; when we have come *through* stage two, and – as thinking adults – assemble the evidence, assess it, and come to a settled and rounded-off world-view that is our own. Until we are at that point we have not yet grown up (1 Cor. 3:1; 14:20).

So if I were to say to you, 'Please describe to me your understanding of life on this world – family, work, relationships, life-purpose, death, where you fit in with the universe' – what would you say? Would your world-view hold together? Could it stand up when the squeeze is on, and life-threatening pressures are bearing down on you? How satisfying and credible is it?

This is hugely important. You are quite right – no one should become a Christian believer at the cost of committing intellectual suicide *....and no one is required to.* True faith can never be a leap in the dark.

What ought to happen is that our minds should catch up with our instincts as we get older. Our *instincts* will tell us that we are definitely more than blobs of protoplasm wrapped around an appetite. But what does our *intellect* tell us about ourselves, about human love, the world, and life, and God?

Christian faith is our response to the evidence! The *fact* of Christ – how do we account for this fact? It's no good saying that he never existed; for that *would* be a leap in the dark! The words he uttered? *Someone* uttered them, because they stare us in the face out of the printed page – who, then? Whoever uttered them was a giant of civilisation.

Whatever our ability to think, we should bend our minds to the stupendous claims of this man. We need to move on from the youth group. So what, as thinking people, are we reading now? When did we last read the Bible on an *adult* level?

Further, when we are intellectually satisfied that this Man is who he claims to be, we cannot leave it at that. We are then required to ditch our pride and bend our wills to his – as Master of the World, and to say, like Thomas of old, '*My* Lord, and *my* God'. That's faith. True, *informed* faith.

FOR FURTHER STUDY: Richard Bewes, *Beginning the Christian Life*, Christian Focus Publications. (ISBN 1-84550-017-2); Melvin Tinker, *The Road to Reality,* Christian Focus Publications (ISBN 1-85792-958-6).

Q.27

How does the Cross have an affect on me?

I know that Jesus Christ 'died for me' but what does that mean?

Someone says, '*Can you get the door?*' They hope that you will go instead of them. If you don't go, they will have to! It's the principle of **substitution**, or – in the case of the Cross – '*penal substitution*', as Bible students term it. Sin has to be punished and someone else has endured that penalty in my place. That person has become my substitute.

In football, to send on a substitute sounds like sending on someone who is 'second best'. Not so at the Cross. Nothing that God provides is second best. Jesus Christ, who is God in human form, had no sin of his own. So only he was qualified to take on the sin of others because he had none of his own to be forgiven. By doing that he broke the barriers that separated us from a perfect God. The barriers that result from sin, the barriers that cause our spiritual death (Rom. 6:23).

Christ came 'to give his life as a ransom *for* (Greek: 'instead of') many' (Mark 10:45). This principle of substitution is the basis of how we reconnect with God. He died *instead of* me. This works out in different ways:

1. The Cross means that a penalty has been paid

The theological word here is *Redemption* (Eph. 1:7). It's the language of **the slave market**. When you bought a slave you *redeemed* them from their previous owner. In our case a price, the sacrifice of Christ's blood, has been paid for us (1 Peter 1:18,19) to release us from our previous lives. In Scripture 'blood', when not mentioned at the same time as the body, means 'death'. So, by his death, Christ became 'a curse for us'; he delivered us from the curse of the law (Gal. 3:13).

2. The Cross means turning away God's anger against sin

The word is *Propitiation*. It's the language of **the Temple**, particularly sacrificial offerings. God's holy opposition to human rebellion brings us all under judgment, we are all as guilty as Adam in turning against God. The story of the Bible is of *God satisfying his own judgment through what his son did*. The English Standard Version has 'propitiation' as the correct translation in such passages as Romans 3:25 and 1 John 2:2 ('He is the propitiation for our sins'). God has to be against us if we are sinful or he ceases to be holy and just. It is *his* righteous anger against us that is turned away by Christ's *substitutionary* sacrifice.

3. The Cross means that righteousness has been swapped

Now the word is *Justification*, and it's the language of **the law courts**. I know I have sinned so how can I be treated as though I had never sinned? Only by Christ taking my place at the Cross and being treated as me, the sinner – instead of us being punished, he is. So now, when God looks at me, he doesn't see me, he sees Jesus' righteousness *given to me*. An amazing truth that is unique to the Bible (see ch. 29; also Rom. 3:21-26).

4. The Cross means relationship restored

Now it's *Reconciliation* [being brought back together], the language of **the family** (Rom. 5:9-11). You can see it in Jesus' parable of the prodigal son (Luke 15: 11-24). For us to be reconciled to God means that Christ has to be 'made sin for us' (2 Cor. 5:19-21). Only through Jesus' sacrifice on the cross is it possible for us to be adopted back into the family of God as his children. Only then can the relationship be put right.

These are four wonderful effects of what Jesus did on the Cross, but the principal rock behind them is 'substitution'.

FOR FURTHER STUDY: John Stott, *The Cross of Christ* (IVP). For the glorious sequel to *The Cross of Christ*, see *Christ's Resurrection*, chapters 50 and 83.

Q.28

What is being 'born again'?

Whenever I see 'Born-again Christians' they seem to be fake, all teeth and smiles. Do I have to be like that?

Don't fall for the media cartoon! The 'new birth' is everywhere in the Scriptures (Ezek. 18:31; 2 Cor. 5:17; Titus 3:5; 1 Peter 1:3, 23). It is in John chapter 3, where Jesus said to Nicodemus, '**No one can see the kingdom of God unless he is born again**' (v.3). Nicodemus had been impressed by Jesus' 'miraculous signs' (v.2), the traditional Jewish belief was that *miracles* would bring in God's reign. In effect he was saying, 'It looks like you're ushering in *the kingdom of God!*'

Jesus, in v.3 shows that although Nicodemus could see the *miracles*, his thinking about *the Kingdom* was wrong; in order to 'see', understand *that*, or enter it (v.5) you first had to be 'born again'.

'How can a man be born when he is old?' asks Nicodemus. It wasn't that he didn't understand the picture language Jesus is using – after all, he was a top professor! It was rather that he was still trapped in an old Jewish mindset – thinking of God's kingdom in political terms; like the glorious kingdom of David in the past. How could the Roman occupied, decaying kingdom of that time *ever* be given a 'new birth'? Nicodemus is saying 'You can no more ask for *that* to happen than expect someone to go back into his mother's womb and start life again. It can't be done!'

But Jesus is very firm. 'No one can enter the kingdom of God unless he is born of water and the Spirit' (v.5). Nicodemus still can't get it (v.9) and Jesus has to put him right. After all, Nicodemus is 'Israel's teacher' (v.10); He should *know* the ancient Scriptures that prophesied all this! So 'water' here is not a reference to Christian baptism – which had only just been started – but a reference *back* to those Scriptures that Nicodemus was supposed to know.

What, then, *were* these Old Testament Scriptures that prophesied of people being born of water and the Spirit – passages that Nicodemus should have known by heart? The obvious passages are Ezekiel 18:31; 36:24-27; Joel 2:28 and Jeremiah 31:31-34. So, sprinkling with clean water is seen as the same as spiritual cleansing and forgiveness, a new heart and the pouring out of God's Spirit – on *all* God's people!

Nicodemus had missed these passages, perhaps he preferred to concentrate instead on triumphant 'messianic' passages like Psalm 2.

Jesus is saying, Nicodemus, you have to *make sense of the new birth Scriptures.* After all, sinful human beings give birth to sinful human beings (v.6) – you need a spiritual rebirth! A new promised generation of the Spirit was coming – a *re*-generation, the evidence around it not so much being triumphalist *signs*, like miracles and political clout, as by a new morality; new desires; a personal *inner* relationship – available for all who repented and trusted in the Lord who died for them (v.14-16). 'You *must* be born again', says Jesus (v.7). He means you!

FOR FURTHER STUDY: See also chapters 33 and 88. A fuller exposition of John chapter 3 by Professor Don Carson is obtainable on audio-cassette from All Souls Tape Library: vestry@allsouls.org.

Q.29

I'm a spiritual failure – am I back to square one?

Since becoming a Christian, I get so down because I fail at the same old sins. I keep thinking that I'll have to go back to the beginning and start again.

No, there's no need to do that. If you are finding it hard, it's a good sign that you're developing spiritually because you're now facing opposition!

Learn the unique truth of **Justification**. Once we accept Christ's saving death for us, we are said to be 'justified' in God's sight (Rom. 3:24; 5:1; Titus 3:7). This is a technical word. You can find it when typing documents on a computer. If you see 'Justify' then it means that you want your column of type to *match up* to a neat line down the side of the page.

It's the same in Bible terminology. How can any of us in the human race *match up*, morally, to God's line, or perfect standard, and so be acceptable to him? It's impossible, because sin – another way of saying it is *falling short of God's standards* – affects every member of the entire human race (Rom. 3:9-20).

It is here that the 'good news' of Christ shines at its brightest. Despite our sins that deserve judgment and hell, God himself has provided a way that we can be *declared righteous* – or match up to his standards of goodness. He has come, as the Son, to take our penalty for our sins on himself. That's what happened at the Cross. By this way **alone** we can be declared to 'match up' to his righteousness.

Justification, then, is more than forgiveness – being let off something you did wrong. If we were simply 'forgiven' (which we are through faith in Christ), there would always still exist the uncertainty of what happens next time we sin. Justification means that if we believe we can be sure – whatever our character – that the righteousness of Jesus has been permanently given to us. This is not the same as being made better people (this is the truth of *sanctification* – John 17:17; 1 Thess. 4:3-7). It's not even that we have been declared *innocent*, and that our file is now clear. Instead we have been *made positively and permanently righteous!* That is Justification.

All true believers let themselves down and sigh over their sins, we desire to be more like Christ. We want to make the pain we caused him as little as possible and seek his forgiveness when we fail him. But that doesn't mean that we need to start all over again. Justification stands for ever – once it has been given.

God's grace is its source. It all stems from his love, freely given [grace]. 'We are justified by grace' (Rom. 3:24).

Christ's death is its means (Rom. 5:9). An exchange has taken place (see ch. 24). 'We are justified by his blood.'

Our faith is its channel (Rom. 5:1). How does it reach *me*? Only as I reach out and thankfully accept in trust what Christ has done for me in his death. 'We are justified by faith.'

God has done it all. No charge can ever be brought against you (Rom. 8:33) – it's God himself who has justified you for ever!

FOR FURTHER STUDY: Regarding the truth of 'sanctification' see chapter 93. Also *Beginning the Christian Life*, Richard Bewes, Christian Focus Publications.

Q.30

Does purgatory exist?

What is 'Purgatory' – and how should we think of it?

Purgatory is the teaching that, after death, there is a place or state of temporary punishment before a soul is safely taken into heaven. It probably began to be spoken about around the end of the second century AD. It became popular among many church leaders and was finally agreed upon by the Greek and Latin churches at the Council of Florence in 1439.

The idea has been a traditional teaching of the Roman Catholic Church and says that when you die there is a place of temporary punishment where souls are purified before they can enter heaven. The idea gained more importance at the Council of Trent in 1548. Purgatory is not hell, but rather a place of purifying before heaven; a state supposedly helped by the prayers and Masses offered for you by the living church on earth.

But, as I understand it, the Bible has good news for believing people. *Purgatory does not exist.*

Advocates for purgatory have sometimes used 1 Corinthians 3:11-15, with its reference to the future fire of testing, as proof – but this passage concerns a future *judgment* for Christ's ministers. There is no connection between the Bible and the notion of Purgatory.

1. If Purgatory exists then Christ's sacrifice was not good enough

Are the sins of believers forgiven or not? That is the issue. A look at Romans 3:24, John 5:24, or Hebrews 9:12 shows that the Bible assures us that our sins are forgiven. All is achieved *once and for all* by the historic death of Christ (Heb. 9:25,26).

2. The idea of Purgatory makes God's forgiveness incomplete

People have always wondered whether their sins can really be forgiven. The rediscovery in the 16th century Reformation that believers in Christ are 'justified' and accepted just as they are (see ch. 27) gave the answer. On the Cross, Jesus called out 'It is finished' (*literally, It has been and remains for ever accomplished*; John 19:30). The penalty of our sins has been paid for, once and for all.

[Article 22, at the back of the old English Prayer Book, says that Purgatory is a 'fond thing, vainly invented, and grounded upon no warranty of Scripture, but rather repugnant to the Word of God' – obviously not a good thing then!]

3. The idea of Purgatory means that salvation is remote

Naturally, a new believer in Christ feels very incomplete and unready for the next life! But it is *this* life, and not some imaginary in-between period, that is the true preparation for your eternal future.

It is a great help to think of salvation like three 'tenses' of grammar. 'I *have been* saved from the 'penalty' of sin by a **crucified** Saviour; I *am being* saved from the 'power' of sin by a **living** Saviour; I *will be* saved from the 'presence' of sin by a **returning** Saviour.' *All of our life,* as Christians, is one of Christ's reliable and powerful salvation, from beginning to eternity!

Q.31

Is healing part of salvation?

Is healing guaranteed? Matthew 8:17 says that healings by Jesus fulfilled Isaiah 53: 4: 'He took up our infirmities and carried our diseases'. Does this mean that – as with forgiveness – we can claim healing at the Cross?

At first sight it could look like that. It's been pointed out that the same Hebrew word is used when the suffering servant 'bore' the sin of many (v.14), as when he 'took up' our infirmities (v.4).

However, to bear the sin of someone implies that you are bearing its penalty *instead of them*. Can you in that sense bear *someone else's illness*? To pay the penalty for someone's sickness doesn't mean anything.

A clue lies in Matthew 8 itself. This whole event of compassionate healing took place at *Capernaum* – the cross of Calvary still lay well ahead. The healings of Matthew 8 illustrate not the Cross but *the Incarnation*. God had become human in a true identification with our lives on Earth. In 'carrying' those pains, Christ was doing so, not as the sacrificial Lamb of God on the Cross, but as the God-Man, who was taking part in our suffering world.

A principle of understanding the Bible is that *Scripture interprets Scripture*. When Psalm 103:3 praises the Lord 'who heals all your diseases' we have to interpret such a phrase in the light of the rest of the Bible (including Ps. 103 itself). Here the language used is that of being saved from a world affected by sin and from the 'pit' of hell (v.4). The same interpretation is given of Isaiah 53:5, 'With his stripes we are healed' – the apostle Peter connects this verse to our being restored from the bad effects of sin (1 Peter 2:24).

On reading the first Christian sermons, in the book of Acts, it is quite clear that it was not healing that was on offer but forgiveness and the gift of the Holy Spirit (Acts 2:38). Healings *did* wonderfully take place – as in Jesus' ministry – but they were firstly 'signs' of the rule of God and pointed to the genuineness of God's messengers.

'Clumps' of miracles seem to mark the beginning of each new phase in God's revelation. The Old Testament spanned about 4,000 years. About fifty miracles are recorded in its pages grouped, firstly, around Moses and the giving of **the Law** and, secondly, around the time of Elijah and the period of **the prophets**. Thirty-seven miracles are written down as being by Jesus at the beginning of **the Gospel** (there were also more unreported cases). Finally, ten recorded miracles feature in the book of Acts with the new era of **the Spirit**. That seems to be the pattern; miracles backing up God's revelation.

This doesn't mean that healings and miracles are ever ruled out at *any* time. Yet even today, reports of miraculous healings usually come from the edge of Christian mission, as God's endorsements of his pioneer messengers. See more on healing in chapter 78.

Q.32

God as Father? I can't get it.

I would like to be a Christian but, coming from another belief, I have never been able to understand how Christians can think of God as a 'father'.

None of the teachings of various religions address God in the name by which Christian worshippers know him best – 'Father'.

1. It is a learnt truth

Get hold of a Bible and look at Luke 11:1-13. Here Jesus is encouraging his disciples to speak to the almighty, all-seeing God, as *Father* (v.2). It was like a bombshell. Earlier there *had* been a 'Father' term – but only used formally, almost as a national title (see Isa. 63:16).

Because we have a mediator in Christ it is a name that no longer puts the believer at a distance from God. It is a breathtaking privilege for followers of Jesus to take him at his word and to come to the heavenly Father – in a relationship as his son or daughter. It means that we are able to speak in an intimate way from our heart. Fascinatingly, even the name *Abba* (similar to our own term 'Dad') is used to address God – both by Jesus and his apostles (Mark 14:36; Gal. 4:6).

2. It is a revealed truth

No one can grasp it without help from outside themselves. Go to all the religions of the world and you find that Christ's revelation of God as an intimate, loving Father of the believer is unique. We can also go further and say that it is *impossible* to understand it until the Spirit of Christ has touched our lives.

If we think that prayer is no more than repeating something you've learnt, or a mantra, then there's still something blocking our understanding. A famous

England footballer once said, 'I turn to God when I need him'. *But if you love someone, do you only go to them when you want to use them?* His words betrayed an ignorance of the day-by-day trusting Father-child relationship revealed by Jesus to us.

3. It is a transforming truth

Jesus drove it home with a humorous little story about a man who wanted to borrow some bread from his neighbour at midnight and got his way by nagging him continuously, despite the neighbour's door being locked and his family being asleep in bed (Luke 11:5-13). The whole point was that God is *not* like the man in bed. He is *not* a lender; his door is *never* shut to his believing children; and to him it is *never* midnight. The punch-line was, *'How much more* will your Father in heaven give...!'

The relationship of the heavenly Father to Jesus is on a different level altogether. For this, see chapters 81 and 83. Until you get to them ask Christ – in your own words – to convince you of this life-changing truth of God as Father – *and he will.*

FOR FURTHER STUDY: *Open Home, Open Bible* video/DVD series, cassette 2, programme 5. Enquiries: vestry@allsouls.org (for USA, www. visionvideo.com).

Q.33

What is 'filled with the Holy Spirit'?

How can I know if I am filled with the Holy Spirit?

Christians are encouraged in Ephesians 5:18 to be filled with the Holy Spirit. All true Christians have the Holy Spirit living in them from Day One of the New Birth (ch. 28). To have Christ is to also have the Spirit (John 14:16-18, Rom. 8:9).

But there is a difference between those experiences of the Spirit that *began* the Christian life, and those that *carry on through it*. From the beginning Christians are **born of the Spirit** (John 3:5); **baptised in the Spirit** – like all Christians everywhere (1 Cor. 12:13); **anointed with the Spirit** (2 Cor. 1:21,22) and **sealed with the Spirit** (for our security and Christ's protection of us – Eph. 1:13, 14; 4:30). After the time of Pentecost the Bible no longer tells a Christian to seek these blessings because they have already been given us when we accepted the Gospel and followed Jesus.

But when it comes to *growth and progress* in our Christian lives we are commanded not to 'grieve' the Spirit (Eph. 4:30); we are to 'walk in' the Spirit (Galatians 5:16); and we are to 'be filled' with the Spirit. If we want to be useful in the service of Christ then this should be a daily, on-going experience. It's a question of *who controls you*. Not (as the New Testament says strongly) to be controlled by wine, but to be controlled by the Spirit (compare Eph. 5:18 with Luke 1:15 and Acts 2:15). First, then, *how* are we filled – and therefore controlled?

There's no technique involved!

First, in daily repenting of your sins at the Cross you can remove those things from your life that block God's fullness in it.

Second, open your life to the Lordship of Christ through your daily obedience. As we read God's word and obey it, so he will fill us (compare Eph. 5:18 with Col. 3:16).

Third, share your blessings with others in Christian service to them. Paradoxically, you will find that the way to be filled up is to give away! Amazingly we feel better and more fulfilled (and therefore filled) *after* a piece of service than before.

How, then, can you know if you are filled? Ask yourself what is important to you:

1. Are you more focused on Christ than on the Holy Spirit? It's the Spirit's work to floodlight the person of *Jesus* (John 16:14). If he is working in your life, so will you be.

2. Are you more focused on taking than on giving. Are you an obedient servant? A giver or a taker?

3. Are you more focused on the moral than on the sensational? The problem with the 'power'-obsessed Corinthian believers was that in moral character they were still like immature babies (1 Cor. 3:1-3). They needed to grow up and focus on how they could give, rather than what they could get for themselves.

4. Are you more focused on others than on yourself? It's always a sign of the Spirit's filling, that we push *others* to the front!

It's a good sign if you can answer those questions with a 'Yes'. And remember, no-one in the New Testament ever claimed publicly to be filled with the Spirit; it was left to *others* to make the observation. So, if someone asks whether you are filled with the Spirit, your reply should be, 'Ask my family; they'll tell you!'

FOR FURTHER STUDY: See also chapter 88.

Q.34

What is the sin against the Holy Spirit?

What is the blasphemy against the Holy Spirit? Why is it unforgivable? Could I have committed this sin and not know it?

It's one of the top questions that people ask; it's worried many people, including those who tend to being depressed. Oddly, though, it's usually the wrong people who worry about it. Jesus said:

> I tell you the truth, all the sins and blasphemies of men will be forgiven them. But whoever blasphemes against the Holy Spirit will never be forgiven; he is guilty of an eternal sin (Mark 3:29).

People wonder, 'What made Jesus say this?' The answer is in the next sentence: 'He said this because they were saying, **"He has an evil spirit"**'. The frightening thing is that it was the religious leaders who had made the accusation that Jesus, by casting out demons, was in league with Satan. They were attributing the works of God to the power of evil – *It is something that reveals more about their character and level of spirituality than they thought.*

Jesus doesn't say that these teachers of the law were guilty themselves (at least not yet!) of such blasphemy but they were in the danger zone. Firstly, he shows the stupidity of someone saying that Satan was casting out Satan (Mark 3:23-26). Secondly, he argues that if he was able to expel demons, it could only be because he had a greater power to that of the Devil (v.27).

Then, thirdly, he highlights the possibility of people who refuse to see the goodness of God, revealed in Christ by the Holy Spirit – and call good 'evil'. What hope have they?

The point is, that it's *the Holy Spirit's work* to open up people's minds. Jesus' name for the Spirit was 'the Spirit of truth' (John 14:16). He went on to say that the Spirit's work was to convict the world of sin, righteousness and judgment (John 16:8). In his next sentence he explained 'sin' in its essence as 'because men do not believe in me' (v.9).

So people who have been privileged with the truth – but deliberately stamp on it – have a basic principle of judgment on them. Read John 9:40,41. They can do this until they come to a point of no return.

This is not rigid legalism, then. It would be a denial of God's nature as revealed to us if he was to attach a terrifying penalty to a single offence. Blasphemy against the Holy Spirit is neither a carelessly-spoken word nor a one-off action. Even lifelong blasphemers and fraudsters have known the experience of forgiveness in late life. No, the 'eternal sin' comes when someone stands the truth on its head and treats as diabolical the wonderful things revealed by the Holy Spirit. In such a case there's nothing more to be done – if they cannot see God's grace held out for them then they cannot believe. They cannot be saved if they don't trust in Jesus. These people are especially in danger of sinning against the Holy Spirit *if they are a teacher of others*.

But this is clearly not your situation. The people who worry about sinning against the Holy Spirit don't need to ask your question. And the people who *should* be asking this question never do.

Q.35

What is 'speaking in tongues'?

How big a deal is it to speak with unknown words and sounds in one's prayers?

The first thing to say is that praying in this way features in the Bible. It also occurs in a number of belief-systems, including Hinduism and even spiritism.

Admittedly, praying in tongues does not feature very prominently in the Scriptures. The Day of Pentecost is unique in the Bible. It was when onlookers heard the Gospel, each in his own language, through the inspired speech of the apostles. It is not repeated anywhere else. The other records we have are of times, both in the book of Acts, and in 1 Corinthians, when the tongues were unintelligible, unless (as in 1 Cor. 12 and 14) there was an accompanying gift of interpretation telling others what was being said.

Thus, out of the twenty-seven New Testament books, only two make specific mention of this phenomenon (unless you include the textually uncertain ending of Mark's Gospel). There's no evidence that Jesus ever prayed in this way. Don't get me wrong, this is not to downgrade a gift intended by the Lord for some of his children (1 Cor. 12: 29,30) – but rather to see it in a proper perspective.

How big a deal? you ask. There's really no big issue about it. If God the Holy Spirit gives to an individual the ability to pray in a special language – so by-passing the usual thinking processes – then it is to be received as a blessing. Note that the Bible doesn't define its value, beyond using the word 'helping' or 'edifying' and goes on to insist that there should be no neglect of praying 'with the mind' *also*.

Problems only happen when the gift gets pushed aggressively, *or* attacked fiercely, in a church fellowship – then divisions can occur. The problem in the Corinthian church was that a 'tongues movement' had been started, dividing the church. We would not have known that the apostle Paul possessed the gift of tongues if he had not corrected the unbalanced Corinthians – saying that he could outdo all of them in this area – he says that he would far prefer to speak *intelligibly* (14:18,19).

1 Corinthians 12–14 is not, then, set against a neutral background and so cannot be *the* definitive passage on spiritual gifts. For that, we would need to look at Romans 12:3-8; Ephesians 4:11-16 and 1 Peter 4:7-11. The passages in 1 Corinthians are given to *correct* an unbalanced church from serious error. Note Paul's frequent use of the word 'but', for example, 'I would like every one of you to speak in tongues [they were doing it anyway] *but* I would rather you have prophecy' (14:5). He uses the same sort of phrase in regard to his own 'gift' of singleness (1 Cor. 7:7).

Everyone doesn't have the same gifts. Use the gifts you *have* been given – and give God the glory.

FOR FURTHER STUDY: Billy Graham, *The Holy Spirit* (Collins), and the *Open Home, Open Bible* video series, cassette 4. Enquiries: vestry@allsouls.org (for USA, www.visionvideo.com).

Q.36

What happens at Communion?

Does a change take place in the bread and the wine during the Holy Communion service? What am I supposed to be thinking, when I take part?

If you read 1 Corinthians 11:17-34 you can see that we can wreck even the wonder of this supper that Christ gave his friends to observe to remember him. *Yet nothing could have been more simple.* 'He took bread...he broke it...."This is my body, which is for you; do this in remembrance of me"...he took the cup...."do this, whenever you drink it, in remembrance of me"' (vv. 24,25).

Jesus never wrote a book. No monument was set up in his name. Instead he left his friends this very simple act of remembrance. These powerful visual aids to the gospel were to represent his body and his blood given for us in death. In this way, Christ's love for us at the Cross has been firmly placed at the centre of the church's memory.

'The Lord's Supper' or 'Holy Communion' is – as these names imply – a time of fellowship. This fellowship is with the once-crucified and now-risen Lord, and with our fellow-believers. It is a tremendous Gospel occasion.

No observable physical change takes place in the Communion elements [the bread and the wine]. They are important for what they *symbolise* – the body and blood of Jesus Christ. As the Church of England Prayer Book declares, '...the sacramental bread and wine remain still in their very natural substances, and therefore may not be adored (for that were idolatry, to be abhorred of all faithful Christians)'.

What, then, does it mean symbolically, to 'eat the flesh' and 'drink the blood' of Christ? It sounds strange to modern ears. A clue to help us is found in the meaning attached to these phrases in the Old Testament. For example,

David the psalmist wrote, 'When my enemies came upon me *to eat up my flesh,* they stumbled and fell' (Ps. 27:2). By that phrase he meant that his enemies would **take advantage** of his downfall. Similarly, he says 'Shall I *drink the blood* of the men who went at the risk of their lives?' (2 Sam. 23:17) about those who obtained water for him at great risk. He meant that he was reluctant to **take advantage** of their sacrifice.

That is exactly how we should understand this picture language of eating and drinking Christ's body and blood – **we are taking advantage of his sacrificial death for us.** We come to the Communion, perhaps with a sense of failure and doubt: *Did he die for me? Does he love me? Has he really forgiven me?* Those visible reminders on the table are saying in a powerful way, 'Yes, he did! Yes, he does! Yes, he has!' It is what theologians call 'dynamic symbolism'. As I receive the bread and drink from the cup, I am feeding upon Christ in my heart, reassured of his saving friendship by the power of those dramatic visual aids.

Q.37

What about those who have never heard the gospel?

If someone from a non-Christian country hasn't heard the gospel then it's not their fault, is it?

Too often this question comes from not seeing the world through 'biblical eyes' in three ways:

1. A view of sin that is not deep enough

The question is sometimes asked as though people who have never heard the Good News are in a state of innocence – and that God somehow *owes* it to them to save them. We mustn't cave in to thinking as though there is a kind of Plan B for these people. There is one plan, for *everybody*.

Does anyone at all *deserve* to be accepted by God? No! The whole world is guilty and has been condemned. No one has any 'right' to be saved because human beings are a race of rebels. It doesn't matter whether you come from a Christian or a non-Christian country, if we have no faith in Christ then we 'are all under sin' (Rom. 3:9).

2. A view of Christ that is not big enough

Jesus Christ isn't just another teacher, like Confucius, aspiring to speak across the ages. He *is* the Creator, the cosmic Christ, who holds the universe together (Col. 1:16,17; Heb. 1:3). He can speak to people's hearts everywhere, and prompt them to seek him (Acts 17:27).

No one, whenever and wherever they live, is beyond the witness of Christ. Psalm 19:4 says that the heavens 'declare the glory of God' and that 'day after day they pour forth speech'. In the New Testament, the apostle Paul uses those same words when writing about *salvation*. He identifies them as 'the word of Christ' and adds, 'But I ask, did they not hear? *Of course they did*

(Rom. 10:17,18). No one can claim that they are not responsible for their sin before God – everyone has been spoken to.

Also the power of Christ's saving death doesn't have a start and finish date, for he is 'the Lamb that was slain *from the creation of the world*' (Rev. 13:8). If anyone is going to be saved at all (BC or AD) it will only be through faith in the Christ who died for the sins of the world – however that message comes to reach them.

3. A view of the Gospel that is not urgent enough

It has been argued that those 'who have never heard' will be judged on whether they acted according to their level of knowledge. This is another way of proposing salvation by sincerity and good deeds – and so is a denial of the Gospel. Go back to the point above – *everybody knows!* It also cuts out the need for urgent missionary activity – frequently an embarrassment to holders of this view.

The church, though, lives by its evangelism (Rom. 10:14,15). By the end of the first century AD, there were churches in Europe, China, India and Africa. Had there been no impassioned missionaries to proclaim Christ's good news, *you* would certainly not be reading this page.

FURTHER STUDY: See also chapter 67.

Q.38

Why does God allow suffering?

There is so much suffering in our world. If God is all-powerful then why does he allow it?

Are we asking the question **in theory** (as an observer) or **personally** (as a sufferer)? *It makes a difference.* When a tower fell, killing eighteen people (Luke 13:1-5), Jesus explained that the victims were no more 'guilty' than anyone else but that unless those around him repented they too would one day 'perish' (in Greek: 'be ruined'). Jesus was saying, 'Listen, let's stop talking theoretically about *their* death, let's talk about *yours*?' Suffering ought to teach us to be humble – one day it will be *our* turn.

Are we asking the question **critically** (as an outsider) or **believingly** (from within the faith of the Bible)? *It makes a difference.* If you are an unbeliever then your mind doesn't understand any purpose for suffering. By contrast, Christ's disciples – though it makes their brains hurt – do see suffering as *a central part of our biblical world-view.* It's built into our framework of thinking.

There are four great Bible supports to biblical belief. John Stott helpfully identifies them in *New Issues Facing Christians Today* (Marshall Pickering, 1999, p.39). They are **Creation**, the human **Fall**, God's **Redemption** in Christ, and the final triumphant **Consummation**, when everything is brought back together. Questions on every issue may all be answered through looking at one or more of these four mighty supports.

When it comes to suffering, we need all four. *Creation* tells us that suffering was not part of God's original order. The *Fall* tells us that, by our sin, as those looking after God's world, we incurred death and pain and all that goes with them. Not only our environment but the whole universe was affected (Gen. 3:17,18). *Redemption* tells us that God has involved himself in our world, lovingly reclaiming us through Jesus suffering at the Cross. The *Consummation* tells us that, while this process of reclamation is not yet complete, we are heading towards a perfected, reborn universe at the end of this age. This inspires us in our service towards the suffering world around us.

Christians can live with challenges like this question once we understand these principles above. If you read Romans 8:18-27 you will see how, because of the Fall, **we ache, along with nature** (vv.19-23; compare Isa. 24:5). We're aching for something better – and it's on the way! So **we ache from hope** (vv.23-25) but the unbelieving world struggles on, *not knowing* there's something better ahead. Christ is our best model to look at, we can find inspiration and courage in *his* sufferings (v.17). **We also ache in prayer,** helped by the Holy Spirit (vv.26, 27) because sometimes we hardly know what to say (Ps. 77:4).

Ultimately it's only the Cross through which we can make any sense of our sufferings (1 Peter 4:12,13). We learn that suffering and 'glory' run side by side – you cannot have the kingdom without trials (1 Peter 5:10; Rev. 1:9). Affliction, then, can lead to spiritual growth and our eventual good (Rom. 5:3-5; Acts 14:22) but we only learn this from the inside, and not always when we are going through suffering (Gen. 50:20).

Q.39

Is everything fixed in advance?

I'm trying to get 'Predestination' worked out. Is everything I do (becoming a Christian, my clothes, my friends, my score at _Halo 2_) decided before birth?

People who support **Determinism** would say 'Yes'; that, although you think you are responsible for your actions, you are only a machine product of genetic inheritance. Such theories excuse people of morality and are dismissed in Professor John Wyatt's magnificent book as 'scientific rubbish and spiritual idolatry' (_Matters of Life and Death,_ IVP, 1998, p.116). We have only to read of the personal Creator in Psalm 139 to expose the lie.

Certain Eastern belief-systems place every event and decision of our lives within a straitjacket called **Fatalism**. If an aeroplane – or a marriage – gets into trouble, this is believed to have been decreed eternally, and must therefore be accepted. Such non-Christian theories deny God of having true relationships, it implies that people are just puppets.

In the Bible there are three great activities of our _personal_ God and Father:

1. 'Predestination' deals with the Christian's destiny
Certainly God predestined the believer from eternity to be 'called', 'justified' and 'glorified' (Rom. 8:29, 30) – but without obliterating our freedom to _'come'... 'receive'....'believe'_ (Rev. 22:17; John 1:12; John 5:24). Indeed some passages combine God's predestination and our responsibility for our actions in one and the same sentence (see John 6:37).

Ultimately predestination is a family secret, recognised only from the inside. We step, by an act of the will, through a gateway over which are the words

'Whoever is thirsty, let him come'. When we look back on the *inside* of the gate we read 'Chosen in him before the creation of the world' (Eph. 1:4). The truth does not lie somewhere in between these great truths, you should not believe one at the expense of the other – *it rests fully on both*. That may not be the neat solution that you want but it is important to recognise that both are true.

2. 'Election' deals with the Christian's salvation

The believer learns that 'from the beginning God chose you to be saved...' (2 Thess. 2:13) and so are to be among the 'elect' who will be collected together by God at the final day (Matt. 24:31).

People are sometimes naturally concerned with the question 'How can I know if I am one of God's elect, chosen for salvation?' The answer is easy (you didn't expect me to say that – did you?), *Christ* is supremely *the* chosen one in whom God delights (Isa. 42:1; 1 Peter 2:4). So you only need to ask yourself 'Have I come to *Christ'* (Cor. 5:17)? If so, because you are now *in him* you (along with him) are 'chosen' (Rev. 17:14). *You are one of the elect.*

3. 'Providence' deals with the Christian's daily life

Providence is not to be confused with **Predestination** or **Election** (let alone any notion of fatalism). Instead it's all about our regular care by our heavenly Father. So, while it is your destiny and salvation that are planned from eternity, it is God's providence over your daily welfare that sets you free to work, dress, plan and decide things – all the while still praying in trusting dependence '*Give us this day our daily bread'.*

Q.40

Who is the Antichrist?

Can you explain to me about the Antichrist? Is this someone who is already here in the world, someone in the past, someone in the future – or is it the Devil?

Antichrist, while not identical to the Devil, is obviously an ally of him. This opponent of God is called by this name only in the New Testament letters of John.

Anti implies 'opposition', and so we find the Good News Bible translating *antichristos* as 'the Enemy of Christ'. But *anti* can also mean 'instead of', so a second line of Bible teaching holds that 'Antichrist' also refers to an alternative, a *rival* to Christ, falsely claiming to be the true Messiah (1 John 2:22). Antichrist, then, looks like a Satanic attempt at copying the incarnation of Jesus – through an evil human personage.

Antichrist is actually defined by denying that Jesus is Christ incarnate: 'Every spirit that acknowledges that Jesus Christ has come in the flesh is from God, but every spirit that does not acknowledge Jesus is not from God. This is the spirit of the antichrist...' (1 John 4:2,3).

Also Antichrist, while ultimately portrayed as an end-time being, is to be preceded in Christian history by the *many antichrists* (1 John 2:18) whom deny Christ in one way or another...

"Some deny his deity, some deny his miracles, some deny his virgin birth, some deny his word, some deny his atoning death, some deny his bodily resurrection, some deny his personal return. Antichrists, the lot of them!" (Guy King, *The Fellowship,* Marshalls, 1954)

This Antichrist figure has other titles in Scripture. The apostle Paul writes of **the man of lawlessness** (or 'the man of sin') – as someone who will oppose the Lord, setting himself up in the place of God (2 Thess. 2:3,4). The last book of the Bible describes **the beast**, who similarly demands universal worship (Rev. 13:1-8). Jesus predicted the coming of a terrifying figure, originally written about in the book of Daniel, known as **the abomination that causes desolation** (catchy title! – Dan. 9:27; Matt. 24:15).

Perhaps the fact that the Antichrist is given these different titles should put us on guard against getting diverted by endless arguments about who exactly he is. A knowledge of Christian history, in addition to the teaching of Jesus, should discourage us from such imbalance. Remember, people seeking a definitive answer always get it wrong! *Our main focus should be upon Jesus himself – not his imitators.*

Ours should be the same principle as that used when defeating financial forgery. We need to be so familiar with *genuine* money – by its appearance, feel and texture – that we more easily recognise the counterfeits. Our energies should be focused, not so much upon the person of the Antichrist, but, by training in the Scriptures, on the *real* Christ! Then, when the antichrists of whatever kind appear, we won't have too much trouble spotting them.

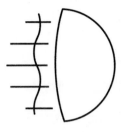

PART THREE
THE BIBLE WE READ

I want to know one thing – the way to heaven; how to land safe on that happy shore. God himself has condescended to teach the way. For this very end he came from heaven. He hath written it down in a book.

O give me that book. At any price, give me the book of God. I have it: here is knowledge enough for me.

Let me be 'homo unius libri', a man of one book.

From a prayer of John Wesley, evangelist,
1703–1791

Q.41

How did the Bible come to us?

What were the languages that the Bible was written in? And how did it end up in its present form?

Broadly, it was Hebrew for the Old Testament, and Greek for the New Testament. As far as the Old Testament was concerned, 'Men spoke from God as they were carried along by the Holy Spirit' (2 Peter 1:21). As for the New Testament, the testimony of Christ's apostles was that what they wrote were 'words taught by the Spirit' (1 Cor. 2:13). Here were books, then, inspired by the Spirit of God. These are not collections of human wisdom but revelations of God's wisdom.

Conclusion: The Bible is a *Library* of sixty-six books, written over a period of 1,500 years, by a wide diversity of inspired writers.

We owe so much to faithful translators. The first outstanding translation of the Old Testament was the Samaritan (400BC). This Hebrew version was followed (in 270BC) by a translation into Greek carried out by seventy Greek-speaking Jews at Alexandria (hence its name *The Septuagint* – Greek for 'seventy').

It is the Septuagint that is usually quoted in the New Testament. Prominent among its many manuscripts are two in the British Museum (*Codex Alexandrinus* and *Codex Sinaiticus*), and one in the Vatican in Rome (*Codex Vaticanus*). As far as the New Testament is concerned, there are also numerous manuscripts (see ch. 47).

A mighty translation of the whole Bible (based on the Hebrew of the Old Testament and the Greek of the New Testament) came into being in the fifth century AD, under the hand of Jerome. It was intended to be a version that all Europe could read so it was in Latin – the common language of the time – this became known as the *Vulgate* (meaning 'common', something for everyone). It helped to mould the culture of Europe over the next thousand years.

Many scholars have worked on other translations. Among them was Baeda (The Venerable Bede, 673–735), who was born in Durham and whose last dying work was the translation of John's Gospel. Even King Alfred the Great was recognised for his work with the Psalms – through his influence the Bible became the basis of English law.

None of this work was without opposition. After the Norman conquest of England education took a back seat and the Latin Bible became largely unintelligible to people. One of the bravest translators was John Wycliffe (1329–1384) who defied the corrupt Roman Catholic hierarchy of the time to produce a new translation of the Vulgate into English. This radical act (once again putting the Bible into the common tongue) paved the way for the Reformation of the church a hundred years later.

The Bible owes its modern form more than anyone to the work of the English reformer and scholar William Tyndale (1494–1536): translating into English from the original languages of Hebrew and Greek. Helped by the invention of the printing press, thousands of newly-translated Bibles were published in the face of relentless persecution. Tyndale was finally tracked down at Vilvorde, near Brussels, strangled and burnt at the stake. Ironically most of Tyndale's work was adopted into the Authorised Version of 1611 (also known as the *King James Version* – after the King who authorised it who was one of those hunting Tyndale down). The 'AV' shaped the English language for three centuries to come.

Be grateful for your own copy of the Scriptures. It came to you through the blood of many martyrs.

Q.42

Who authorised the Bible?

If it was the church that finally decided which books should be included in the Bible, then isn't the church the top authority?

No; the Bible produced the church, not the church the Bible. The issue is 'What caused a book to be accepted within the 'Canon' of Scripture?' (Greek: *kanon*, 'standard' or 'rule').

For the **Old Testament:**

1. They had to be books that were recognised by Jesus Christ as infallible 'Scripture' (Matt. 5:18). In John 10:35 Jesus didn't have to explain what he meant by 'Scripture', though elsewhere he did refer to its different categories (law, prophets, psalms) as pointing to himself (Luke 24:44; Matt. 24:37). All was to be believed and obeyed.

2. Books that were recognised by God's people *because of their impact.* God's people will always recognise God's voice (John 10:27). Jesus clashed with the Pharisees for *adding* their traditions to the Scripture; yet all were agreed that the Old Testament Scriptures were God's word.

3. Books that were recognised by the New Testament. It is significant that the New Testament features hundreds of quotations, concepts and ideas from the Old Testament. (Only two are from the body of books known as the Apocrypha (Jude v 9, 14) but they seem to be used in the same style as the apostle Paul's quotation from a Greek poet in Acts 17:28. The Apocryphal books were perceived to be on a lower level than scripture but of help to the believer (see ch. 43).

What rules were used to include books in the New Testament Canon?

1. Books that are Christ-centred in their emphasis. It was inconceivable to the early church that the Gospels, for example, which focused so much upon the life and death of Jesus, could have any lower place than that given to the Old Testament scriptures.

2. Books that are apostolic in their teaching. Jesus exclusively promised guidance to the apostles 'into all truth' through the Holy Spirit's inspiration (John 16:13). The result of this was the New Testament (1 Cor. 2:12,13). Peter tells us to include Paul's writings with what he calls 'the other *scriptures*' (2 Peter 3:15,16). He didn't have to explain what he meant.

3. Books that are faith-building in their effect and thus to be read in the congregations (John 20:30,31; 1 Thess. 5:27; Col. 4:16; 1 Peter 2:2; Rev. 1:3). When the Christian scriptures take hold of the thinking of masses of people, they have the effect of 'stabilising society, without sterilising it' (historian T.R. Glover).

The books of the Old Testament were largely accepted by AD70, those of the New Testament were assembled by around 30 years later and accepted by the end of the second century. The drawing of a line around them discouraged forgers and breakaway religious groups.

So no one really 'put' the books into the Bible; they put themselves in, because of their innate quality. No council by itself could have conferred authority upon the books; they already had it. *It is an in-built authority, not one given by someone else.* If an art lover says of a painting, 'This is a genuine Renoir', it doesn't make the painting authentic; *it was already authentic.* It is the same with the Scriptures; we can only recognise them as such...and live by them.

Q.43

Is the Apocrypha Scripture?

What place do the books of the Apocrypha have in the Bible?

In chapter 42 we learnt that the books of the Old and New Testament selected themselves.

But what of the Apocrypha? The *Apocrypha* (the word means 'hidden things') is a collection of Jewish books that, over the centuries, has not gained general recognition as being on a level with the books of either the Old or New Testaments. It includes such books as *The Wisdom of Solomon, Ecclesiasticus, 3rd Esdras, Baruch* and *1st and 2nd Maccabees*.

The Roman Catholic Church did not come to consider certain apocryphal books as being part of inspired Scripture until a ruling in 1546. It was at a time of great tension within the church and some point out that this decision could be explained as a reaction to the reformers rejection of these books as part of scripture, rather than a ringing endorsement.

Across most of Judaeo-Christian history the apocryphal books have been left outside the canon of Scripture, although many parts of them have useful knowledge in them. Nevertheless, at the close of the first century AD, the Jewish synod of Jamnia took place. Then it was clearly recognised that while the books of Proverbs, Ecclesiastes, the Song of Solomon and Esther rightly remained as accepted Scripture, there were others that were definitely on a lower level and should not be classed with the canonical books.

The Christian church has taken the same view. Although Jerome did include them in the *Vulgate* (see ch. 41) he classed these documents in a separate category of their own (*libri ecclesiastici*). To his mind they were useful for edification, but were not the definitive, inspired truth of God. They were different from what he called the *libri canonici* – the canonical books.

A final word concerns the books of what is generally called 'The Apocryphal New Testament'. These take the form of a random assortment of books that, through imaginary reconstruction, attempt to fill in gaps in the Bible narrative – for example; Jesus' early years and Pontius Pilate's story. Additional 'Gospels' are attributed to Peter, Thomas, Paul and Andrew. It indicates how highly Christ's apostles were thought of that so many fanciful documents were attributed to them. They have been rejected as scripture largely due to inconsistencies with the 66 canonical books, historical inaccuracies and the obvious pushing of a particular theological trend of the day.

There is a principle to learn from these apocryphal documents, many of which were characterised by various heretical overtones. As Tertullian put it (at the turn of the second century) – **Truth precedes forgery.**

NOTE: Episcopalian and Anglican worshippers are sometimes puzzled by the mention of 'the First and Second Book of Esdras' among the Bible books listed in Article 6 of the Book of Common Prayer. This was only another way of describing the canonical books of Ezra and Nehemiah that follow one another. All the historic reformed churches are agreed on the content of the Canon.

Q.44

Is the Bible a unique authority?

Why should we believe in the inspiration and authority of the Bible?

The basic answer is 'Give it a try'. See what effect it has upon you by a steady reading of its contents. The evidence for the Bible's divine inspiration will be found within its pages – rather than from external literature. After all, books written about the Bible will all be out-dated within ten or fifteen years. So look within! Having said that there are good reasons to trust your Bible.

1. Its character implies a divine origin

First, **its unity;** the Bible was written over a period of 1,500 years by many different authors. Despite this the unifying theme of Salvation in Jesus consistently shines through (Luke 24:25-27). Secondly, **its prophecy;** we have only to glance at, for example, Isaiah 7:14, Micah 5:2, Zechariah 9:9 or Psalm 22:16,17 for the point to register. If someone says something will happen, and it does, then you will trust them.

Thirdly, **its purity;** here is a book that has inspired inventive creativity, self-sacrifice and the highest ethic ever known. Evil is unashamedly described ...as is the answer to evil.

Fourthly, **its honesty;** the Bible is not afraid to show the failings of its characters. It does not try to make super-heroes out of Abraham, Moses, David or the apostle Peter. Nor does it attempt to smooth over difficulties or apparent discrepancies in reporting. It is not the sort of books humans would produce!

2. It claims to be of divine origin

'All Scripture is God-breathed (2 Tim. 3:16), 'men spoke from God as they were carried along by the Holy Spirit' (2 Peter 1:21). Couple those references (which are of the Old Testament Scriptures) with such passages as 1 Corinthians 2:13,16; Revelation 1:1 and 2 Peter 3:15,16 (where Paul's writings are bracketed with 'the other *Scriptures*') and a consistent picture emerges of both Old and New Testaments claiming that their ultimate author is God the Holy Spirit.

If you are given poetry to read, and are told that this is a book of free verse, you would be mad to try to make the poems rhyme. You would read it as it sets itself out to be. So it is with the Bible. *Thus says the Lord... The word of the Lord came... God spoke by his servant...* We take note of the fact that Jesus, in his attitude to the Old Testament, **revered it** (Luke 16:17), **believed it** (Matt. 19:4,5; Mark 12:36) and **gave it supreme authority;** *above reason* (Matt. 22:29) and *above tradition* (Mark 7:13). To him, the Scriptures were *the* great source of authority to any situation (Luke 24:25).

3. Its impact proves a divine origin

This is the practical clincher. There are critics who would say, 'Go on then, *prove* that the Bible is the Word of God'. Our reply to them should be, 'No, *you* prove it. Take it and read it – and see if it doesn't alter your ethics, your mindset and your whole relationship to the universe. See if it doesn't make the person of Christ real to you.'

FURTHER READING: Colin Peckham, *The Authority of Scripture*, Christian Focus Publications.

Q.45

Has there been no further word from God?

Is God still speaking today? Why was the Bible not added to, as time went on?

It's *Jesus Christ* who provides the answer to this question. The Bible claims that God has nothing definitive to say to us greater than what he has said to us through Jesus Christ. Hebrews 1:1,2 expresses it perfectly: 'In the past God spoke to our forefathers through the prophets at many times and in various ways, but in these last days he has spoken to us by his Son...'

That explains so much – **no one is ever going to improve on Jesus!**

What God has to say to us reaches its goal in Christ and the message of his chosen apostles. We are not going to discover any new teachings that are better than that. In Jesus, God has said all that he wants to say to the human race, there is no extra revelation to follow, no additional prophetic word. Jesus himself warned against future claimants to some new messiah-ship even if they performed miracles by way of proof (Matt. 24:23-26; Luke 17:23); you are not to listen to them.

It is not that everything has stood still since the first century! Christ is alive and active: guiding his church in fulfilling his will and extending the kingdom of God. Hence the excitement and the growing sense of momentum imparted to Christians of every century.

But there is something about the 'givenness' of the Bible that means it is not to be added to. Timothy, the protegé of the apostle Paul, was to *keep the pattern of sound teaching,* and to *guard the good deposit* (2 Tim. 1:13,14). The Bible is not an interesting collection of human insights that can therefore be added to. Instead we read of *the trustworthy message... the sound doctrine... the faith that was once for all entrusted to the saints* (Titus 1:9; Jude 3).

Quite evidently this is a library of books that is not to be tampered with. Its end perfectly matches its beginning; it starts with the creation and closes with the *new* creation; it originates in a garden and terminates in a garden *city*; a tree features in the opening pages of the Bible and the tree of life is present in the final pages. In this way the two covers of the Bible can be bent back on themselves so that Genesis meets Revelation and Moses shakes hands with John. How could anyone think of adding extra material to such a perfect entity? This is the book of God and we can only pity those who have fatuously claimed 'We wrote the Bible so we can *rewrite* the Bible.' A divine judgment rests on those who would add anything to, or take anything away from, the last book of the Bible (Rev. 22: 18,19). It's one that we should bear in mind with all scripture.

Whilst there is nothing more to be revealed, there is plenty more to *learn*. This is the excitement of Bible study, theology and scholarship. We will never reach the stage when we sense that we have mastered God's book. We are able to explore its contents until the end of time!

Q.46

What about the errors?

I get discouraged by people who are more knowledgeable than I am insisting that the Bible is full of contradictions. How can I answer them?

'Show me one!' I said to the man who tried the same thing on me. 'Er, well...', he replied, 'How about that bit where it says God helps those that help themselves?' Of course there is no such Bible sentence and I told him so. My friend had another try...and then had to give up.

What do we do with Bible difficulties?

1. Deal with them humbly. Of course we would be insincere to say that we encounter *no* difficulties in the Bible. In it the eternal and infinite God has spoken his mind and it would be strange if we, finite humans, found the reading of this book to be a doddle!

When we encounter Bible difficulties our first assumption ought to be that the problem is more likely to be with our imperfect understanding rather than in what God is telling us. *Nothing* that God has spoken can be feeble or mistaken! The Holy Spirit is the person who wrote it so there is no-one better to ask for help in your private daily reading and study!

2. Don't deal with problems alone. Others before us have studied the Scriptures – and studied them in depth. We can be grateful for the great Reformation principle that every believer can study the Scriptures for themselves (without the church having to tell them at every turn what they are to believe – *the right of private interpretation*) but that doesn't mean we have to re-invent the wheel every time. It's good to ask for help and consult more experienced students of Scripture. We can be like the Ethiopian of Acts 8:31 who realised his inability to understand '...unless someone explains it to me'.

We can also learn one to one in small study groups... through the regular exposition of the Bible at the church gathering, from Bible commentaries and video seminars with *Open Home, Open Bible* or the *Book by Book* video course. Understanding the Bible is not like a private correspondence course or attending night school! It is a fellowship exercise.

3. Deal with them patiently. It is fascinating how Bible difficulties can melt away – given enough time for us to grow in our understanding. When baffled by an apparent Bible error it is sometimes best to simply make a note of the difficulty and then mentally to shelve it for a period while we continue in study. It may be a year or two later, resulting from our own further reading, hearing a sermon or going to a Bible study, when suddenly the answer to the problem drops into our mind – 'Of course!'

FOR FURTHER STUDY: For actual examples of Bible difficulties, see the last section of the original, unmixed version of this book or the forthcoming 'Top 100 Difficult Bible Passages'. Also the video study series *Open Home, Open Bible* and *Book by Book*. Enquiries: vestry@allsouls.org (for USA: www. visionvideo.com).

Q.47

Are the Gospels reliable?

I have heard the argument that the Gospel books of the New Testament were changed after they were written. Can you comment, and can you suggest a helpful book?

Of course; when we hear a statement questioning the authority of the New Testament Gospels we are wise to ask its critics for their basis in putting forward such a sweeping theory. We should immediately take them up on a number of specific instances. 'Now, the account of Zacchaeus in Jericho… was that tampered with, can you tell me?' 'The Sermon on the Mount in Matthew 5–7… how much invention went into that?' 'What about the Lord's Prayer?'

Sometimes people suggest that Jesus never said the things he is reported to have said. We should push them a little by asking, 'Oh! OK – who *did* say these things that stare us in the face from these documents; sayings that have gone round the world, shaped our vocabulary and brought comfort and strength to millions? Because whoever did say these things was a giant – and I would want to follow *that* person to the end of the world!'

In point of fact it is wonderfully reassuring to the Christian, to know that **there are several thousand Greek manuscripts, containing the whole, or at least part of the New Testament.** It is very rare to have originals for documents of this age but the sheer volume gives authority to the contents. The oldest and most significant of these manuscripts go back to the mid-fourth century AD – an astonishingly early date. In addition there are a considerable number of fragments of much earlier copies still, going back to hundreds of years earlier.

The evidence is that the New Testament was complete by AD100. For example, Ignatius the martyr quoted from the Gospel of John, and his death is reckoned to have taken place around AD107. The bulk of New Testament scholarship today dates the writing of the Gospels before AD70 (the year of the destruction of Jerusalem – their argument being that, if they had been written afterwards, such an important event would have influenced the content).

Thus it is clear that the Gospels were in circulation during the lifetime of people who had seen and met with Jesus. As Professor F.F. Bruce commented: 'It can have been by no means so easy as some writers seem to think to invent words and deeds of Jesus in those early years, when so many of his disciples were about, who could remember what had and what had not happened'.

There is every reason for accepting the New Testament documents as reliable.

Again, from F.F. Bruce: 'No classical scholar would listen to an argument that the authenticity of Herodotus or Thucydides is in doubt because the earliest manuscripts of *their* works which are of any use to us are over 1,300 years later than the originals!'

FURTHER READING: F.F. Bruce, *Are the New Testament Documents Reliable?* (IVP).

Q.48

What about the 'later' bits in the Bible?

What of those sections in the Bible that people suggest should not have been there at all? How does this affect our view of the authority of the Bible?

First some reassurance: there are such sections, but (a) they are not many and (b) none of them affect any basic Scripture teaching. They are passages that, on examination by Bible scholars, do not feature in the oldest and most reliable Bible manuscripts. Usually they will have become incorporated later into the main text of Scripture through what is called a copyist error.

There is an example in John's Gospel chapter 5. Here is an account of the healing of the disabled man at the pool of Bethesda. In any modern version of the Bible you will find that verse 4 is missing from the main body of the passage. It has been taken out of the older King James Version and has been relegated to a footnote in all modern Bible versions. The now relegated verse 4 reads as follows:

> From time to time an angel of the Lord would come down and stir up the waters. The first one into the pool after each such disturbance would be cured of whatever disease he had.

'That reads rather like a bit of local folklore', I hear you say. And in all probability that is exactly what it was. In fact, when the archaeologists discovered the pool of Bethesda in their excavations of 1876 they found all five 'colonnades' (mentioned in verse 2) and with them a faded fresco showing an angel troubling the water – obviously connected with the legend. The archaeologists also found a subterranean stream that would occasionally bubble up and disturb the pool.

I think we can see what happened. A scribal copyist would have been in the habit of including a little bit of 'commentary' of his own in the margin of the passage that he was copying – not as part of the main manuscript but simply as an interesting observation. This is what probably happened with the angel legend. Later still, a further scribe inadvertently copied what was originally this margin note into the main text of the passage. There it remained, until, by comparing manuscript with manuscript, Bible scholars were eventually able to unravel what had happened and straighten out the text. At that point the passage was purified of the extraneous margin note.

There is a similar uncertainty about the last twelve verses of Mark chapter 16. They simply are not found in the oldest manuscripts and so are now treated as a footnote.

However, when you look at the nature of these few additions, the overwhelming message is the wonderfully consistent harmony that characterises the vast bulk of the biblical manuscripts.

This is part of the adventure and challenge facing lovers of the Bible. It is *because* we believe that what God originally has spoken is to be believed and received as his inspired Word that every possible care has to be taken to establish the true text.

Q.49

Is the Bible really 'God's Word'?

Is the Bible, in itself, the Word of God, or does it only 'contain' God's Word, as some people say?

No, the Bible *is* the Word of God. Once we claim that it only 'contains' the Word, then *humans* have taken the place of supreme authority. What of the Bible is God's Word and what is not is up to *us* to determine!

Such a view could be descibed as one of:

1. 'Limited' inerrancy. On this view the Bible is said to be true and without error *on matters of salvation and theology* but that if you use it in the field of science or history it becomes unreliable.

Can you see the flaw in the argument? For example, 'God created the heavens and the earth.' Is that theology or science? It's both! *We can't disentangle the two categories.* Again, 'Christ died for our sins.' Certainly salvation is present in that sentence – but so is history! Once we start to place our own arbitrary limits on God's Word then it degenerates into the word of humans. You can make it say what you want it to say.

But then, in the opposite direction there is:

2. 'Literalistic' inerrancy. Difficulties occur when we fail to recognise when the language is figurative, visionary or poetic. This happens when readers of the Bible mistakenly apply an artificial literalism to every statement. Confusion can also arise if we insist that twenty-first century standards of computerised precision be applied, for example, to the numbers in the Bible, or to its chronology when *its human authors were plainly not intending this.*

In preference to the above interpretations there is what I will call:

3. 'Original' inerrancy. Our right approach lies in the fundamental principle that has to be applied to *any* document: **A text means what its original author meant.**

Question: Did the original authors *intend* at times to give round numbers, rather than precise figures? See, for example, the 24,000 who died (Num. 25:9) as against 23,000 (1 Cor. 10:8). Presumably the *exact* figure was between the two.

Question: Did the inspired authors *intend* to select the events and persons included in their books? If so, leaving out certain dates or historical events should not concern us. Bible history is necessarily selective – it is *interpreted* history with a specific purpose in view (John 20:30,31). If Matthew *intended* to highlight the theme of God's kingdom by editing and grouping together a collection of Christ's parables in his thirteenth chapter, rather than presenting them in the order or the place where they were told, then no critic should complain. These are Gospels, not log books! Do you believe that Christ only told a parable once? No! He said them often and sometimes with different details for his audience!

If a writer intended to give an *approximation* of an Old Testament quotation no problem! Did some writers intend to put down only a *summary* of reported speech – or do we imagine that Peter's sermon at Pentecost (Acts 2:14-36) lasted less than three minutes?

Have we got it? The Bible is God's unique, inerrant Word, but we are wise to treat it as it was intended to be read – and not to press its authors into a mould of our own making.

Q.50

Are the actual words of the Bible inspired?

Are the actual words of the Bible inspired or only the general sense? I ask because of the differences between the Gospel writers, for example, about the resurrection of Jesus.

Well... once we take away the words there's nothing left! If the Bible is inspired at all then we must hold to what is called *Verbal Inspiration.*

Let's take those resurrection accounts. Don't be thrown by little differences. One angel features in Matthew but two in Luke and John. But is Matthew just concentrating on the angel who was speaking? When did the women visit the empty tomb? 'Just after sunrise', says Mark. 'While it was still dark' writes John. It was similar at the Battle of Waterloo in 1815. The reports varied *according to your own point on the field.* When did it begin? 'At ten o'clock' said the Duke of Wellington, 'at half-past eleven' said General Alava, 'at twelve' according to Napoleon and Drouet, 'at one' stated General Ney. They were all right because the battle developed over that time to different points.

This illustrates the strength of having four Gospels. Some critics seem to insist that they should be identical – in which case they are asking for nothing more than photocopies! In fact all four Gospels *complement* each other. You want an example? How about making sense of Easter Day!

Early on Sunday the resurrection happens – it's marked by an earthquake – and then an angel descends and rolls away the stone from the tomb (Matt. 28:2). Mary Magdalene, Mary the mother of James, and Salome then come to the tomb (another group of women follow with the spices). Mary Magdalene arrives first (John 20:1,2), sees that the tomb is open and *immediately* rushes to inform Peter and John.

The *other* Mary and Salome now reach the tomb, see the angel (Matt. 28:5) and are told to tell the news to the disciples. They go, then the *further* group of women with the spices (including Joanna) approach, see two angelic figures and are reminded by them that Jesus had predicted his own resurrection (Luke 24:1-7).

Meanwhile, Mary Magdalene has alerted Peter and John, and they set off for the tomb (John 20:3,4), running – with Mary trailing behind. By the time Mary has arrived, Peter and John have already been into the tomb and have gone (John 20:10). Now Mary, on arrival at the tomb, stays weeping (John 20:11). She sees the two angels who ask her why she weeps. She then has the encounter with the risen Lord (John 20:14).

Whilst this is happening the *other* women are seeing the rest of the disciples, but their report is dismissed as nonsense (Luke 24:11). It's probably then, on their way back to the tomb, that Jesus meets them and they worship him (Matthew 28:9).

Some time later that day the risen Christ meets with Peter alone (Luke 24:34; 1 Cor. 15:5); also with the two travellers to Emmaus (Luke 24:13-35) and then, later still, with the entire group of the disciples, except Thomas (Luke 24:36-43; John 20:19-25).

If you believe in verbal inspiration, you will do the spade-work of study to get the whole picture. If you don't, you won't bother.

Q.51

Can you make the Bible say what you want it to?

I sometimes hear different interpretations of Bible passages from speakers at Christian meetings. Are they all valid?

No, they are not. If I was to write to you and suggest that we meet next Wednesday at 3 pm 'at the courts' obviously there *could* be more than one meaning to my words. If you didn't know me you might be wondering 'Does he mean the *law* courts or the *tennis* courts?'

However, if you knew me even a little bit, or had had the opportunity of reading *other* letters I had written, you would know for sure that it was the tennis courts that I had in mind – no mistake! **In no way would I have dreamt of intending you to make two or more meanings out of my reference to 'the courts'.**

Yet this is the madness of the approach to the Bible made by some modern teachers. They seem to forget that when people write something down for others to read then *one meaning,* and one meaning only, is intended. We hear it said that 'we can no longer talk of the theology of the Bible, only of its theolog*ies*'. It is even claimed that every text of the Bible is 'infinitely interpretable'!

No! – we **must remember the principle spelt out in chapter 49 – that a text means what its author meant.** So, there is only *one* real interpretation of a Bible passage and it is through a growing knowledge of the rest of Scripture that we can understand the meaning of what we are reading. We are to establish – as John Stott has clearly put it:

The natural meaning – without twisting words.

The original meaning – without bending the author's intention.

The general meaning – without ignoring what the rest of Scripture says.

When looking at the early church it's clear that there was common agreement between both apostolic leaders and their hearers of what the Gospel message was. There were plenty of false teachers at hand but the New Testament letters show total consistency in combating their errors. If any *alternative* Gospel interpretations surfaced, they would be exposed as 'a different gospel – which is really no gospel at all' (Gal. 1:6,7).

'Whether, then, it was I or they', said Paul of his colleagues, 'this is what we preached, and this is what you believed' (1 Cor. 15:11). Notice Paul's four pronouns – *I... they... we... you* – there was common acceptance of 'the trustworthy message' (Titus 1:9) among both preachers and hearers! Paul was writing about those things that were 'of first importance' – the death, burial, resurrection and appearances of the risen Christ (vv.3,4). Evidently there was no disagreement about the meaning of the Gospel or of *the* interpretation. There is no reason at all why that should not remain the case today – at least in those churches that submit themselves to the apostles' teaching.

Q.52

May a Bible story be a legend?

Is it possible that some of the Bible accounts – such as that of Jonah – should be interpreted not as factual narratives but as parables, or even as inspiring fables?

Some people have held that this could be so. To investigate we need to look at an example so let's take up your example of Jonah. The first thing to look at is 'Why is the person saying this? What is the real reason?' Usually such ideas are themselves based on what someone wants to believe or a bias in their thinking rather than on looking at what the passage means at face value. We need to ask some searching questions. First, *what kind of literature* are we dealing with? Second, *what was the intention* in the mind of the author? Third, *how does the rest of Scripture* interpret the passage?

The parable, or legend, theory falls down on all three counts. When Luke, in the New Testament, gives us Jesus' parable of the Good Samaritan it's obvious from the start that it is a parable – despite the fact that Jesus uses place names and that Luke never tells us that this is a parable. *One basic point is made and there is a punch line* 'Go and do likewise.' There is no such pattern in Jonah. The story is actually quite involved. It reads like a verbatim report of something that historically took place.

We also note that in 2 Kings 14:25, the prophet is historically *named* as 'Jonah, son of Amittai, the prophet from Gath Hepher' (compare Jonah 1:1). So he is a real person. The clincher comes in the New Testament where Jesus speaks directly of 'the sign of the prophet Jonah' and draws a specific parallel between the experience with the great fish and his own death. He also speaks about the repentance of Nineveh's inhabitants as a real event. They would be there at the final judgment, he says (Matt. 12:38-42).

The book of Jonah, then, is a story of facts and isn't a parable. The great fish? Of course that has exercised the minds of many critics! It sounds unbelievable. Thoughtful readers of the Scriptures have accepted the account as historical long before John Ambrose Wilson reported a similar incident in which the crewman of a whaling vessel was swallowed by a sperm whale off the Falkland Islands in 1927. When the whale was finally killed three days later, the crewman was found inside, still alive. (*Princeton Theological Review,* Volume 25, pages 630-642).

We shouldn't *need* the findings of such outside sources to reassure us of the Bible's truth. If so, human researchers and archaeologists have taken over the place of supreme authority (see ch. 53). It is essentially the Bible that authenticates and illustrates its *own* pages as we compare Scripture with Scripture.

Many have been the times when critics have dismissed accounts in the New Testament as 'midrash' (legendary Jewish commentary) but the structure, style and openness of the Biblical writers show that these narratives are a part of time and history.

NOTE: Regarding the book of Jonah, see the six 15-minute programmes available in the *Book by Book* video series. Enquiries vestry@allsouls.org (for USA: www.visionvideo.com).

Q.53

Should I spend time looking at stuff from outside the Bible?

How far can knowledge of outside history, local detail or archaeology fill out and complement my understanding of the Bible?

There have been many Bible students who were magnificent researchers, archaeologists or historians. Among them were Donald Wiseman, E.M. Blaiklock and T.R. Glover. They have thrilled generations of Bible readers with their discoveries. For instance, it is wonderful to visit the site of Capernaum today, and to see what's left of the synagogue that a devout Roman centurion had built for the Jewish locals at the time of Jesus (See Luke 7:1-10).

How do we know this? Because onto one of these slabs of stone had been carved two stylised eagles – *the emblem of the Roman tenth legion*. This would have been regarded as an idolatrous symbol to put on a place of Jewish worship... except if the synagogue had been funded by the generosity of someone in the Roman military. In this remarkable way he left his fingerprints for all posterity to see.

The Israeli authorities dug up a first-century Galilean fishing boat in the 1980s. I happened to be in Israel a week later and was able to see and photograph the boat while it was still at the lakeside. It was 28 feet long. Why, I thought, this just *could* have been the very boat that Jesus was asleep in during the storm on Lake Galilee! Discoveries like these excite us.

It is the same with historical research. For years it had been claimed by sceptics that King Belshazzar of Babylon never existed: they maintained that it was *Nabonidus* who ruled Babylon at that time? Then further research revealed that Belshazzar was made *co-regent* of the country by his father Nabonidus in 556BC while Nabonidus was away, campaigning in central Arabia (source; the Nabonidus Chronicle).

The great caution about historical and archaeological research is this: in no way can this serve to prop up belief in the truth of the Bible. We do not actually *need* such research to tell us that the Bible is, after all, true! For example, the collapsed walls of Jericho have not yet been discovered. I asked a Christian archaeologist in Israel whether this affected his belief in the truth of the account in Joshua 6. 'Oh! Not at all' he answered. 'I believe the story. What we do in such a case is simply hang around. The walls are somewhere in this area. They'll turn up!'

In our study of the Scriptures we are wise, then, not to rely on what is called 'the historical critical method', **for if we do, then archaeology and historical records have been put in a superior authority over that of the Bible.** Then the tendency is to interpret the Bible through what we discover outside of its pages. If we have faith *we only need the Bible* because it interprets itself. These 'outside helps' are there as useful *illustrations*, but no more than that. They come in the category of what I call 'thrillmanship'.

Q.54

Where is the Bible's power?

If the Bible is the powerful Word of God, why is there not more evidence of that power around today?

For a long time there has been, at least in the West, a sapping of confidence in the Scriptures. It began well over a century ago with the rise of a new theology, particularly from Germany, that looked at Scripture from the starting point of disbelieving its authority. It was not long before this negative material drip-fed its way into the universities, the schools, the media and also the church.

We are grateful now for a new breed of theologians who are well equipped to deal with 'liberal theology' but the damage from the past is still having an effect. In the West, after World War II, the voice of influence moved away from the church to the *theatre and the cinema*. These became the places where the serious issues of our lives were explored.

Then it got worse, as the entertainment media became the workshop for today's big themes much of the church, in its frantic desire to get back an audience, attempted in an amateur way to cash in on the role of public entertainer! *We have seen a neat exchange of roles.* The biggest-selling tapes at Christian conferences are often those of the speaker with the biggest range of funny stories.

This shows up our loss of confidence in the power of the Bible – even amongst those who publicly embrace it. They do not carry it with them and they fail to study it systematically. Instead of relying on explaining the Bible's meaning they rely on personality, music, humour and marketing techniques to gain their attention.

As a result, *experience* has become more important to the church than understanding the Bible. We now have two new forms of religious existentialism (believing only what you can experience): one European, and negative, the other American, and positive. Both are equally dogmatic and both are equally destructive. We have to grapple with both.

The European model of existentialism would take as its watchwords, '**We can't believe that today**'. The implication is that what I can experience, see and 'prove' is the judge of what is to be believed. 'We've never seen a miracle, so miracles do not occur.'

American religious existentialism, which takes a positive form, would have as its watchwords, '**The Lord has told me**'. The implication is that what I feel, sense and experience has a higher authority over all else, including the Bible. If, for example, my religious experiential feelings tell me that it is all right to enter into a sexual relationship, that's what I will do, ignoring the Bible's ban on sex outside marriage.

There is an answer.

The apostle Paul gives it in 1 Corinthians 4:6, '**Do not go beyond what is written**.' We come to the Bible *humbly* – knowing our own understanding can be fragile – and *prayerfully* – accepting that we need to depend on God the Holy Spirit, the author of this wonderful Book.

Q.55

Must I read my Bible every day?

People tell me that the traditional daily 'Quiet Time' with the Bible and prayer isn't found anywhere in the Bible and is only a piece of evangelical legalism. Is it all right to not do it every day?

The trouble with agreeing with this is that if we stop reading the Bible our spiritual temperature becomes so low that we don't realise that *our spiritual cutting edge is already blunted.*

That means that we get into difficulties over Christian truth and our doubts increase about the Bible itself. Then it becomes unfashionable to take the Bible to Christian meetings. We can even reach the point when a meeting is in progress (even a Bible study) – and no one has a Bible! The sins that we once tried to overcome we now just give in to – *and yet we still fail to connect our feeble discipleship with our neglect of reading the Bible.* Now isn't it strange that if we read our Bible again on a regular basis that within days we notice a difference in our lives!

No, a daily quiet time is not a legally binding duty: instead we should look on daily Bible reading as a personal daily delight. 'When your words came', said Jeremiah, 'I ate them; they were my joy and my heart's delight' (Jer. 15:16). We fall in love with Christ – and we find ourselves *wanting* to read the Scriptures – because they lead us to him (John 5:39).

Should it be morning or evening? Again, there is no legally binding rule. I've seen people reading the Bible on the London underground. Some find that the evening time, before bed, suits them better than the morning. Whatever you choose you may find that when illness or bereavement strikes then your Bible reading and prayer may well fade out for a period.

For most believers, however, the words of the American Bible teacher Henry Ward Beecher applies: **The first hour of waking is the rudder that guides the whole day.**

David the Psalmist knew this. 'I rise before dawn', he exclaimed, 'and cry for help. I have put my hope in your word' (Ps. 119:147). This sounds like a habit!

Isaiah knew it too. 'The sovereign Lord has given me an instructed tongue, to know the word that sustains the weary. He wakens me morning by morning, wakens my ear to listen like one being taught' (Isa. 50:4).

That sounds to me like *every day*! The apostle Peter exhorted his readers to receive God's 'pure spiritual milk', so that by it they might 'grow up' in their salvation. He then adds, 'As you *come* to him, the living Stone....'. The Greek of the text indicates that they were to *continue* coming, in this way (1 Peter 2:2-4) – it was a regular thing.

Let daily Bible reading and prayer be like meeting your girlfriend or boyfriend. The Danish philosopher, Søren Kierkegaard, once observed, *A believer is surely a lover; yea, of all lovers the most in love!*

FOR FURTHER STUDY: Read Chapter 77.

Q.56

OK, I'll read the Bible – but how do I listen to God?

People say that I must spend time listening to God. But how can I know that it is his voice I'm hearing?

You have hit on a desperately important issue. Throughout history people have claimed that God spoke to them and then have performed stupid actions on the basis of what proved to be a delusion. It sounds mystical, even a little super-spiritual, to say that I have heard the voice of God. The problem is that we only have the authority of the person who claims this that it is so. *Where is the independent check that this is true?*

Among the worst examples were the ill-fated Christian 'Crusades' of the Middle Ages. What madness prompted Pope Urban II to ignore what Jesus said to call for military action against the Muslims in a sermon at Clermont in 1095? The crowd's shouted response, 'God wills it!' became the slogan that spread shame upon the face of Christ's mission of love to the world.

God wills it... God spoke to me. How many times have such sentiments been used, publicly and privately, to prop up an ill-thought out programme, unwise relationship and empty-headed scheme? All that grief could have been avoided if only the Scriptures had been studied seriously.

We *should* listen to God, and the sure and certain way to do it is to be humble when we come to him with the Bible open in front of us. As we read, we pray – expecting God's Holy Spirit to help us understand and apply the words where we need it! If I am reading Hebrews 3:7 I am not just reading about a warning given to someone centuries ago, I read, 'So, as the Holy Spirit says, **"Today, if you will hear his voice,** do not harden your hearts."' I read God's Book – and I become aware, 'He's speaking to *me!*'

Look up Ephesians 4:21. Many modern versions translate it, 'Surely you heard *of* him' (Christ). But the King James, and other more accurate versions, have it correct. The word 'of' is not present in the Greek text – the true translation is 'Surely you heard *him*'.

'Really?' we ask. 'But those Ephesian Christians were far from the land where Jesus lived and taught. They only heard Paul and his friends!'

Not so. They were listening to preachers *but they also became aware that another voice had taken over.* They heard Jesus speaking to them through what they heard and trusted!

It happens today. I've lost count of the number of times when people exclaim at the end of a sermon or Bible study, 'That was for me; Jesus was speaking to *me*!'

If you really believe that the Lord speaks to us through the Scriptures – applying them by his Spirit personally and practically – then you have to take the Bible more seriously. Do you carry it with you every day? In your pocket or backpack? Small pocket Bibles can be expensive but why not put one on your birthday or Christmas list? And do a great deal more reading, and therefore plenty of listening!

FOR FURTHER STUDY: Video programme: Cassette 1, programme 4 of the *Open Home, Open Bible Series* features Joni Eareckson Tada, speaking with Paul Blackham and Richard Bewes on this important topic.

Q.57

Should the Bible be banned?

I read in a newspaper that someone was trying to obtain a court ruling that the Bible breaks the law by what it says. What is the Christian answer?

Opponents of Jesus Christ will go on trying to ban the Bible until the end of time; we should not be surprised or alarmed – any pretext will do!

The notorious Ugandan president, Idi Amin, once declared that the word *Israel* should be deleted from the Bible on the grounds that it was a racist book. A prominent homosexual campaigner once admitted that in any hotel bedroom containing a *Gideon* Bible, he would tear out the pages where homosexual activity is condemned.

There are always individuals who poke around in the Scriptures, trying to discover passages they can say are immoral by today's social consensus but we should ask the critic 'Have you ever been into a pornography shop, and if so, how many Bibles did you see on display?'

Society in the end is likely to side with the historian G.M. Trevelyan. He wrote that the effect of studying the Bible in the seventeenth century *'upon the national character, imagination and intelligence for nearly three centuries to come was greater than that of any literary movement in our annals or any religious movement since the coming of St Augustine'.*

Certainly, there are Bible passages that, if they were read in public, would make us wriggle with unease because the Bible deals with life as it is. Categories that the apostle Paul described as 'fruitless deeds' that were 'shameful even to mention' (Eph. 5:12). The same could be said of what are sometimes called the *imprecatory psalms*, which include real and passionate human sentiments like 'Break the teeth in their mouths, O God!'

We should not think that such passages are any less 'inspired', or less pure, than the rest of God's Word. They all form part of the total inspired revelation. A revelation which puts its entire weight behind goodness and purity. The 'impure' events related in its pages are there as part of the realistic picture given us of fallen, unredeemed humanity.

Would we have wanted the Bible in another guise: one of schmaltzy, sweet, 'religious' varnish – made safe by church-approved phraseology?

Maybe the campaigner seeking to ban the Bible hasn't stopped to think that if you did ban the Bible then you would also have to ban most of the world's most famous literature – Dostoevsky, Tolstoy, Milton, Bunyan and Walter Scott... book after book. There are 300 Bible quotations in Tennyson's works alone. There are over 500 biblical allusions in the writings of Shakespeare. Even Karl Marx's *Das Kapital* would have to be changed, and his other writings, if the Bible disappeared. At a stroke, the artistic works of Michelangelo, Raphael and Leonardo da Vinci would be reduced to unintelligibility, together with great music from Beethoven, Mozart, Handel and U2!

The apostle Paul, chained like a criminal in prison, wrote 'But God's word is not chained' (2 Tim. 2:9). And it never can be – even if people think they can do it.

Q.58

Should I read nothing but the Bible?

Is it best if my Christian reading is confined to the reading of the Bible alone?

If your question implies what I think it does – that at heart you want to be, as John Wesley once expressed it, a person 'of one book' – then I want to encourage your desire strongly. In your own times of quiet with the Lord, let it be the Bible that you focus on exclusively. We need our spirits to be fed by the 'pure spiritual milk' (1 Peter 2:2), rather than secondary material; by the Bible *itself*, rather than by *echoes* of the Bible.

This does not rule out using helpful Bible notes or commentaries for daily reading – provided that the writers of these aids are consistently pointing the reader back to what the scripture says – rather than to themselves.

Let your understanding of the Bible be as clear and simple as it can be. Some people mark their Bible; in the margin, they write down what they have discovered; or they may use highlighters to mark what they consider to be especially helpful. It's fine to do this, but my strong recommendation is that you should never use such a marked Bible *for your daily devotional reading* because then you will always focus on the things you have written, rather than what new thing the text may have to say to you. We need to come to the pages of the Bible with a fresh attitude each time – as though we had never seen the bit we are reading before!

But there is another point to make. The Baptist preacher C.H. Spurgeon once commented on Paul's request for books in 2 Timothy 4:13: Spurgeon preached **'Even an apostle must read. He's inspired, yet he wants books! He has seen the Lord and yet he wants books! He's been caught up to the third heaven,**

yet he wants books!' This tells us that there is every reason to be buying and reading Christian books if we want to grow as mature, thinking believers – and to set apart time to read and study them.

Even a busy man like King Alfred the Great did this. Back in the ninth century he was the first truly great Christian King of England. He put himself and his courtiers through school. He would set apart eight hours for sleep, meals and recreation, eight for public duties, and eight for reading, study and prayer.

If top scholars have given the best part of their lives to the understanding of God's Word, then we should be glad to benefit from their studies. Commentaries on the Bible itself, books on Christian teaching and ethics, books on how to share our faith with others, books that help us deal with modern controversies and other religions; Christian biographies, church history and missionary thrillers – all of these are going to *help*.

Go to your church bookstall, or to a reliable Bible bookstore, and build up your own Christian library.

Q.59

What about 'atrocities' in the Bible?

Was Moses no better than Stalin because of the slaughters that we read about in the Old Testament? Is the morality different between the Old and New Testaments?

No, the morality in the Old and New Testament is exactly the same. The problem with some people is that they would like it both ways when it comes to God's morality. They complain, 'Why doesn't God *deal* with the people who committed the atrocity of 9/11?' and yet also say, 'How cruel of God to wipe out the Amorites at a stroke!'

If justice for human wickedness is delayed then that is because of God's patience – but it will come. In the words of Von Logau's poem *Retribution,* translated by the American poet Longfellow…

> Though the mills of God grind slowly,
> yet they grind exceeding small.

That is exactly it. 2 Peter 3:3-9 refers to both The Flood of Noah and the fire of Judgement Day *in making the same point*; that God is not slow in bringing retribution upon wickedness; it will happen. At the same time he is also 'patient …not wanting anyone to perish, but everyone to come to repentance' (2 Peter 3:9).

At the time of the Flood the Lord declares, 'My Spirit will not contend with man for ever' (Gen. 6:3) – or, to put it another way, God will not always be patient. God feels 'grief' and 'pain' over sinful humanity and his retribution at the time of the flood was universal – but so was the message of saving grace that started with Noah's family and has since reached everywhere.

What were the Amorites like? In their day they were notorious for their child sacrifice and lack of principles. Living in their society was like living in hell. Why were they not wiped out before then? God explains to Abraham that 'the sin of the Amorites has not yet reached its full measure' (Gen. 15:16). Hundreds of years passed in which the long-suffering Lord was gracious to the Amorites before his terrible vengeance overtook them (Num. 21).

The principle of these judgments is the recognition on a public scale – for all to see – that wickedness will be overthrown. Even Israel is not exempt. If necessary, God would use a heathen nation to bring judgment upon His own people. **Yet these fearful judgments in history were really warnings to people of the most terrible fate of all – banishment for all eternity to the hell of final separation from God.**

The judgments of the Bible are there to give us an *Education*; the lesson is that sin will always meet its just desserts; they give *Comfort* to all who long for justice; they give us a *Warning* – as we look back to the past (1 Cor. 10:11), and as we look forward to the end of time (2 Peter 3:11,12). You should be glad that the Lord does not ignore wickedness **but be thankful too that he spares us from final judgment by enduring the worst 'atrocity' of all – the Cross, where the sinless Christ underwent the agony of the judgment and retribution that should have been ours.**

Q.60

Are you 'inside' or 'outside' God's blessings?

I am aware of a kind of 'racial selection' process running throughout the whole Bible but on what basis is the blessing given? And is it fair?

You are basically asking, 'If God started with Abraham, the "father of all believers" who inherits his blessing'? Jews claim Abraham on the basis of the genetic line through Isaac; Muslims on the strength of the line through Ishmael. Where does that leave Christians?

But these claims, and others like them, are untrue to the Bible. God's selection for blessing is simply not based on genetics – otherwise the rejected Esau could stake as good a claim as anyone. We are not to think of this as an ethnic, racial or cultural issue (for then it *would* be unfair) but as one involving *faith*.

Look at the Bible like an old-fashioned sandglass (the type which people used for timing their boiled eggs) wide at each end and narrow in the middle.

At the 'top end' of the Bible, the scale is massive: 'Let us make man in our own image' – and our human story begins. But then we trace a narrowing-down process, as God selects the people through whom his love will be made known to the world. Down to where the Old Testament takes up the story of Abraham, and a single family, the basis of a chosen nation – the people of Israel.

It then narrows this nation down further as four-fifths go into captivity because Israel failed to be a faithful light to the world. We are left with Judea, a tiny kingdom no bigger than Yorkshire or New Jersey.

Then it gets smaller still, because even that little kingdom's people get carried off into captivity. Although the exiles do eventually return it looks as though Israel's light has finally gone out. The Persians, Greeks and finally the Romans occupy the world stage. Israel is just another racial tribe whose land is fought over by others. There is just a small 'remnant' of faithful people by the end of the Old Testament.

Four hundred years pass and we enter the New Testament. The sandglass has now narrowed down to thirteen individuals – a Rabbi and his disciples. Surely it couldn't get any smaller? But it does. The drama boils to a crisis – one member turns traitor; another becomes a coward; the rest scatter – to leave us at the narrowest point of the sandglass with *one person*, Jesus, who dies in solitary degradation.

And everything in the divine kingdom and plan hangs upon his faithful sacrifice and death. At that point *he is* 'Israel'; *he* is the chosen people; *he* is the faithful fulfilment of the age-long Covenant – One Person!

From then on, the sandglass gets wider again as the message of love and forgiveness, centring in Christ, travels out in ever widening circles, Jerusalem, Judea, Samaria… and the ends of the earth (Acts 1:8).

Christ is **the** chosen one (Isa. 42:1; 1 Peter 2:4). As men and women of every ethnic background and culture put their *faith* in him, they too may be said to be 'chosen in him' (Eph. 1:4), and to be true children of Abraham. That is the story of the Bible.

PART FOUR
THE WAY WE BEHAVE

We recognise a tree by its fruit; and we ought to be able to recognise Christians by their actions. The fruit of faith should be evident in our lives, for being a Christian is more than a matter of making sound professions of faith. It should reveal itself in practical and visible ways.

Indeed, it is better to keep quiet about our beliefs, and live them out; than to talk eloquently about what we believe, but fail to live by it.

Ignatius of Antioch,
c. AD35–107

Q.61

Does Christianity have the highest standard of ethics?

It seems to me that all the different religions have something to offer. How can Christianity lay claim to providing the highest ethic?

The answer has to be *look at the founder*. It's important because 'religions' historically often compromise the ideals of their founders. They either give up on their principles, change what their founder meant or distance themselves from the founder – especially as character defects become known, often from their own records. We must go back to the original prototype, and ask, 'Can *this* figure credibly lay claim to being the all-time Teacher of the world?

In such a quest, character is absolutely vital. For a teacher of physics, or a football coach, character is not seen to be the biggest issue. They may have a range of dubious sexual relationships or violent temper but, provided they are reasonable citizens, it is their success in teaching or on the pitch that people look at.

This is not so when it comes to candidates for the role of light-bearer for all humanity. Their character, more than anything else, must come under the microscope. You won't be able to advance their claim if they have a scant regard for human life, have an assortment of wives and dubious relationships, are piling up money or if they fail to become personally involved in the suffering world around them.

In the case of Christianity, sadly, there have been plenty of deviations from the original prototype – particularly by those who have found it profitable to operate under Christ's banner while forming their own power base (whether materialist, militarist or racist). Some religious practitioners will call Jesus 'Lord' only to be told by him at the last judgment 'I never knew you. Away from me, you evil-doers!' (Matt. 7:23).

So, back to the prototype. It's here that I become convinced of the validity of Christ's claim to be 'the way, the truth and the life' (John 14:6). Other religious leaders would say, 'I have discovered the answer; now follow this teaching' but none of them claimed to *be* the answer, as Jesus did. And none of them said, as Jesus did, 'Follow *me*'.

It is the intrinsic, magnetic *goodness* of Jesus that has drawn millions of us – unattractive characters as many of us are – to his feet. Unlike some leaders, he has not won our loyalty by giving us wealth or coercing us by force. He has a totally clean record in the area of intimate human relationships. He betrays no hint of a remote 'other-world' detachment from human calamity. The beginning of hospitals and the care of leprosy sufferers (whom no one else dared to touch) derive from him. The lifting of oppression from women in society, although long resisted even today, is due to Christ and *the* behavioural feature that marks out the true Christian – the love of one's enemy – is one we owe to Jesus.

It was well said by the fourth-century Christian leader, Ephraem of Syria, 'There never was a King like this before!'

Q.62

How dangerous is wealth?

What are the moral issues about having, or making, lots of money?

First of all we should recognise that Christianity doesn't present us with a biblical economic theory or an ideal political system to live by in this world. But it does give us a viewpoint, a perspective on *life*, which helps us to cope with money and to manage it. Here is an example:

> Command those who are rich in this present world not to be arrogant nor to put their hope in wealth, which is so uncertain, but to put their hope in God, who richly provides us with everything for our enjoyment. Command them to do good, to be rich in good deeds, and to be generous and willing to share (1 Tim. 6:17-19).

It is clear that there is a great danger to our psyche attached to having lots of 'stuff'; Christians are also to show a true solidarity with the poor; yet, there is nothing wrong with wealth in itself (NB although it does make it more difficult to enter heaven. How difficult? As difficult as threading a camel through a needle – that's how difficult!). Poverty is not always the mark of the believer's spirituality, it is not God's will that poverty should be the rule of life across the world.

However, 'Wealth is like a viper', said Clement of Alexandria at the turn of the second century. Richard Foster of our own time gets close to this opinion, with his claim that money has a spiritual, even a demonic character of its own (*Money, Sex and Power*, Hodder and Stoughton). Perhaps this view fails to take into account the difference between 'money' and 'mammon' (*the love of money*). A power so great it is almost like a person itself (see Luke 16:11, KJV and 1 Tim. 6:10).

The debate about wealth creation has been a long one. Max Weber in *The Protestant Ethic and the Spread of Capitalism* (1904) maintained that the biblical outlook of Protestantism enabled a person 'to see in his ordinary daily work an activity pleasing to God and therefore to be pursued as actively and profitably as possible'. Weber maintained that the ethos of Protestantism promoted, as nothing else could have done, the spirit of the entrepreneur, and for that reason wealth creation was to be found largely in countries with a Protestant heritage. This is how we got the often-used phrase 'The Protestant Work Ethic'.

Weber was then challenged by R.H. Tawney in *Religion and the Rise of Capitalism* (1926). While Weber saw wealth creation as one of the positive results of the Protestant view, Tawney attacked not only capitalism for its failure to provide fairness in society but also Protestantism for perverting the Christian message of poverty and charity into a gospel of 'success'.

Tawney was not entirely right. For it is obvious that Luther and Calvin, to take two earlier Protestant leaders, disapproved of profit-making as something worthy in itself. The characteristic emphasis of all early Protestant teaching about wealth was moralistic – with the stress on charity, rather than self-indulgence. John Wesley advised a neat summary in the eighteenth century, 'Make all you can, save all you can, *give all you can.*'

We still need to be on our guard. All too easily a productive, biblical world-view can be spoilt by the Fall – *it is then that mammon takes over.* On the other hand, when wealth has come into the hands of true Christians, the benefits can be wide-ranging indeed.

Q.63

What is meant by 'spirituality'?

People say things like, 'What are you doing about spirituality at your church these days?' What is really meant by this term?

In 1883 the top blew off the volcanic island of Krakatoa in Indonesia. The explosion was heard 3,000 miles away, and the tidal waves reached Cape Horn, 8,000 miles distant. It was the most stupendous explosion ever recorded in history.

Krakatoa is a kind of spiritual parallel to what happened in our world through the death and resurrection of Jesus Christ. The great difference is that, while Krakatoa was destructive, the Cross and Resurrection created the greatest ever shockwave of hope and confidence. Its tidal waves are still being felt, everywhere. It is the 'epicentre' of all Christian experience.

And Christian experience is what we mean by 'Spirituality'. Wakefield's *Dictionary of Christian Spirituality* describes it as 'those attitudes, beliefs and practices that animate people's lives and help them to reach out towards super-sensible realities'.

I tend to use the term 'Christian growth' rather than 'Spirituality', for we are really looking at those influences that *centre us on, and develop us in* the life of Christ. The grace of **God** is our foundation; the death of **Christ** is where our attention should focus, and the everyday relationship with the living Christ by His **Spirit** is what moves us on. Yes, effective Christian living involves all three persons of the Trinity.

The problem with some spiritualities is that they really just focus on *ourselves.* The worship hymns that are chosen make it obvious. Too many of them contain echoes of the Bible, but their main theme seems to be 'Look what I have now I know Jesus' or 'Aren't we wonderful?'! It is the same with some activities that can create a self-obsessed illusion of mystical 'holiness', without actually dealing with our sinful characters.

Colossians 2:16 – 3:17 is a useful passage. See if you can spot the four 'with Christ's' of 2:20, 3:1, 3:3 and 3:4 and work on them! In this chapter, the apostle Paul condemns the rituals and mystical experiences that caused people to *lose connection with Christ the Head of our faith* (2:19). Instead there was an impressive-looking set of religious disciplines that despite looking super-spiritual were really 'based on human commands and teachings'. You can be only one degree off of your course, and everything seems OK at first, but in ten years' time you will be miles from where you should be – and never know it.

At the base of spirituality is Christian fellowship (3:12-15) and 'the word of Christ' (3:16) to protect and build us. Elsewhere we learn how to build on this through prayer and sharing together in the Lord's Supper.

From my childhood, ours was a spirituality built on Bible stories, daily meditation on the Scriptures, the Christian family (and family prayers), the reading of books, prayer meetings, the importance of missionary work and, as we found when in East Africa, suffering. I cannot understand why, in numerous books on 'Spirituality', **this last ingredient is conspicuously missing. Acts 14:22 and elsewhere tell us that to suffer is *essential* (see ch. 38) for growth.** We are, after all, following the way of the Cross – not the way of the Candyfloss.

Q.64

What about forgiving people who don't repent?

Is it biblical to forgive those who show no remorse for their actions?

It is the love of one's enemies that distinguishes the true disciple of Jesus Christ from someone following a set of moral rules.

In Burundi, at the height of its violent troubles, an African Christian was facing the guns of his enemies.

'Before you kill me', he said, 'may I have permission to say a few things?'

'Say it quickly.' They said.

'First,' he said, 'I love you. Second, I love my country. Third, I will sing a song.'

In their mother tongue, he then sang all four verses of the hymn which begins, *Out of my bondage, sorrow and night; Jesus I come, Jesus I come*. And then the shots rang out.

This African Christian was simply following the example of his leader, from a saying which has stamped itself upon the world's consciousness, while he was on the cross 'Father, forgive them, for they do not know what they are doing' (Luke 23:34). The words were to be echoed by Stephen (Acts 7:60) – the first of a long and honourable list of martyrs.

Such attitudes come from working out the Lord's teaching in the Sermon on the Mount: 'Love your enemies and pray for those who persecute you' (Matt. 5:44).

The New Testament emphasises the *attitude* we should have, one that reaches out towards our persecutors. I remember a minister friend of mine speaking movingly on television from his hospital bed after having been attacked by intruders in his own house. He explained that he felt no resentment towards those who had beaten him up.

But your question asks the difficult issue of how far forgiveness should go toward those who show no repentance. All too often someone who has been on the receiving end of an attack is asked *Have you forgiven them?* Put just like that, it is a shallow question.

Sometimes it places an additional burden on the victim; for instance when a rape victim is advised, 'You cannot recover until you have forgiven your attacker'. The wrong person has been placed in the dock.

Jesus' words help us: 'If your brother sins, rebuke him, and if he repents, forgive him' (Luke 17:3). Commenting on this passage, John Stott adds 'and only if he repents. We must beware of cheapening forgiveness ...If a brother who has sinned against us refuses to repent, we should not forgive him. Does this startle you? It is what Jesus taught' (*Confess your Sins*, Hodder, 1964, p.35).

The reason is that real forgiveness implies restoration of the relationship. You can't go back to where you were with someone if they are unrepentant over what they have done. As John Stott observes, 'A forgiveness, which bypasses the need for repentance, issues not from love but from sentimentality'.

The attitude of being *willing* to forgive (or even being willing to be made willing) costs you emotionally. But God is not distant when we need help because at the Cross, a man died for our own forgiveness. Realise that – and a revolution of love can take place.

Q.65

Can euthanasia be an option for a Christian?

Is it not only humane, but compassionately Christian, to follow the medical trend in places like Holland towards assisting in the termination of a life not worth living?

The division between right and wrong can look paper-thin, even blurred, when you base your decisions on isolated and emotional cases. But if you saw someone high on a bridge, convinced that life is not worth living, about to jump to their death, your instinct would be to try and stop them.

What, then, of a society 'which quietly encouraged the depressed, the inadequate, the isolated or the disabled to take their own lives; where doctors made available lethal mixtures for their patients; where suicides were left to get on with it. What kind of a society would that be? Would we wish to be members of it?' (Professor John Wyatt, '*Matters of Life and Death*', IVP, 1998, p.195).

Most civilised people would say 'No'. Your question mentions Holland, where voluntary euthanasia has been legalised. Already there is evidence that non-voluntary euthanasia is now being performed, in situations where a life has been declared to be not worth living. This causes unease.

It is only possible to look at the main reasons for Christians to challenge euthanasia:

1. There is a difference between treatment decisions and value-of-life decisions. It is not for a doctor to pronounce whether someone's life is futile; only whether the treatment is futile. And even then, if the treatment is withdrawn, it should be because the treatment is valueless, *not because the patient is valueless.*

2. There is a difference between removing suffering and removing the sufferer. It is the difference between curing and killing. The 'hippocratic oath', enhanced by Christian teaching centuries later, was a pledge made by doctors to use treatment only to help the sick – no more. In part it says 'I will not give poison to anyone, though asked to do so, neither will I suggest such a plan'. *It was written down because doctors can be influenced, just like anyone else.*

3. There is a difference between valuing someone for who they 'once' were, and valuing them for who they always are – and eternally will be. God has said about the masterpiece of his creation 'Whoever sheds the blood of man, by man shall his blood be shed; *for in the image of God has God made man*' (Gen. 9:6).

4. There is a difference between being an individual and being part of a shared community. God designed us to live in community with others, just as he does. We are designed to depend upon each other so for someone to opt out – *or be opted out* – is a blow struck at the identity of the whole family. It is no answer for the doctor to say, 'There is nothing more we can do for you'. One answer is the development of effective pain care, another is the development of the hospice movement (begun by Christians in Britain by the way) – a service that is virtually unknown in Holland.

Christians find suffering difficult – but it is built into our world-view. It has no purpose or makes no sense in the mind-set of unbelievers; hence their problem with it.

FOR FURTHER STUDY: *Matters of Life and Death*, John Wyatt, IVP, chapters 9-11.

Q.66

Is punishment for eternity?

I can't see that it is justice for people to get everlasting punishment for what may be only a few years or decades of sinful actions.

You can look at this in a number of different ways.

Firstly, on a purely human level, would we question the rightness of putting away someone who – in a couple of seconds of raging fury – had committed murder? I think not. The action might be over very quickly, but the repercussions would last for a long time. Murderers are sometimes put away for 'Life'.

Secondly, let's not minimise the nature of sin. Life is not a matter of balancing up good deeds against bad deeds. We do not start from neutral: we start in a state of rebellion. On the road of life we do not face a fork ahead of us with the choice between the good way and the bad way. Instead the Bible teaches that we are *already on the wrong road* (Rom. 3:23). The real picture is of us being stuck on a motorway, in desperate need of an exit road at the side, so that we can escape to safety.

The Bible tells us the story of God providing the very escape route that we need at great and painful cost. It is an exit clearly marked with signposts to help us leave our hell-bound course. The 'signposts' include the warnings of prophets, sacrificial pictures of future events, Bibles, churches, preachers, videos and Christian books. They are all pointing to the exit ramp provided by the Cross. **If people are to miss the way of salvation, provided by the death of Jesus, they will have to go past all that without noticing it!** God has done everything necessary to get our attention and bring us to safety.

We are shallow in our thinking about sin if we equate it only with a number of individual sinful acts. Our real situation is that, as fallen beings, every moment we live and breathe is in a state of rebellion against God. Our sin and sinful nature makes us unfit to spend eternity in his presence – something has to be **done** to deal with our nature so that we can be brought safely to salvation.

The wonderful good news is that this has happened. God has opened up an escape route through the saving death of Christ and we need no longer be guilty before him. Christ has taken on the burden of our guilt in his own suffering love – a substitute in our place (2 Cor. 5:21; Gal. 3:13). It is a free gift of his love.

Naturally, this is not automatic. *God inhabits Eternity. Do we want to spend it with him?* It would obviously be quite illogical for someone to expect to have everything to do with Christ in the next life, when they have completely ignored him in this. If you live without God in this life then hell is just the confirmation of your wishes for the next.

Ultimately that is *the* sin that will inevitably take a person to their eternal destruction. If we by-pass the signposts, and finally ignore Christ's dying love for us, then we shall miss the one way of safety that he has provided in himself.

Q.67

Wouldn't it be better for unbelievers if we didn't have missionaries?

If it is the rejection of Christ that brings judgment, would not an individual, or society, have been safer without the missionaries telling them about Jesus?

Two corrections: one – we are all under judgment already; two – no one is beyond the reach of Christ's voice (see ch. 37). That is the apostle Paul's argument: *'Did they not hear? Of course they did'* (Rom. 10:18). The problem is that, one way or another, we **have** heard the voice of the cosmic and eternal Christ, and if we refuse that light, we are in darkness.

In your question you are logically saying, 'I myself would have been in a *safer* position if the good news of Jesus had been kept from me. It would have been safer if Britain could have been left under the spiritual leadership of the Druids. People in Europe, Africa or Asia were only exposed to greater peril when the early missionaries risked their lives to bring the Christian message to them – *It would actually have been safer if Christ had not come at all.'*

Let's see where the flaws are in this argument:

The Gospel does not create judgment – it lifts it. *It deals with the judgment that the whole human race already lies under.* Without God's saving action – the death of Christ for our sins – we are all without hope (Eph. 2:12). The one and only way of removing the judgment over us was through the coming of the Gospel and the preaching of its messengers.

We must realise that **those who are without the Gospel are not in a state of innocent neutrality.** No, they actually know they are in trouble but are without hope. We sometimes hear the shallow argument that it was a pity to disturb the primitive traditions and cultures of entire societies by bringing to them the 'alien' Christian message. The assumption is that these societies were happy and contented in a paradise of their own. *But it never was paradise. Life in most primitive tribes was brutal – and short.*

Missionaries have often been criticised for going into Africa along the route carved out by the railways and commercial agencies of the British Empire. This ignores the fact that it was the missionaries who held the key to the eventual freeing of the Africans from the dominating colonial interests. As the BBC documentary historian Jeremy Murray-Brown has written:

Their [the missionaries'] message implied freedom from the ignorance of past centuries; freedom from the thraldom of malign spirits; freedom from the barriers to human progress imposed by tribal custom; freedom from the restraint on social and economic life requited by untamed natural forces. **Such a liberation of men's spirits must finally lead to a demand for personal and political freedom. The missionary gospel carried within it the seeds of decay to the imperial order itself.** *(Kenyatta,* George Allen and Unwin Ltd, 1972, p.41)

The implication from this is that you, and I, should take up our missionary responsibilities to others immediately – there is no time to lose. If there had been any other way, outside of the Gospel, by which humanity could have been made 'safe', Jesus would never have come to die for us.

Q.68

What makes a church a 'sect'?

Any church can fall into error. At what point, though, does false teaching turn a church into a sect?

An identikit of a sectarian teacher is likely to show up in one or all of these five tendencies:

1. The truth-warpers. Gross and blatant error can usually be recognised instantly by most Christians. However, sects advance by means of telling part-truths – ideas that float on apparently 95% of true doctrine. A basic topic found in the Bible, such as the eternal Sonship of Jesus Christ or the resurrection of the body, will be taken and given a twist in a new direction.

2. The sheep-stealers. Because the sects have no true spiritual power, because they rest on distorted beliefs, they have to ride on the backs of those churches and evangelists that know and preach the truth. The sects cannot really evangelise. All they can do is *proselytise*; hovering on the edges of Christian fellowships and student groups and using them as convenient sources of contacts. The membership of sects often consists of untaught Christians.

3. The side-trackers. *Novelty* is the attraction. 'You think those sermons and Bible studies are boring? Here's something fresh that you never knew was in the Bible!' The way of the side-trackers is, first, to *dazzle*; secondly to *distort*; thirdly to *deceive* and fourthly to *divert*. Often it is the side-issues, the 'curiosities' of Scripture that instead become the central area of their teaching. The result is that unwary believers are seduced into leaving the mainstream of Christian living, and become locked in a side-water.

4. The peace-breakers. Sects will never see themselves as *part* of a wider fellowship. They will never be found in inter-church get-togethers, or take part in shared outreach programmes. They are IT! So, if they ever gain a foothold in a Christian student group they will never be content to follow the existing leadership. Rather, the tendency will be to undermine the leaders and infiltrate the membership with a view to taking it over. If they get into a church it won't be long before divisions are set up and unity breaks down.

5. The power-brokers. The sects tend to rely upon a central, powerful and charismatic leading figure – or an all-dominating leadership circle – usually accountable to no one but themselves. All the arrows of attention are pointing *inwards* towards the leadership. Total loyalty is insisted upon. If the structure is like a church then the money, and even the homes of its members, as well as their decisions and relationships will be controlled by the leadership.

Such groups existed in New Testament days – Yep, there's nothing new here! The apostles warned their readers (Col. 2:8; 2 Tim. 3:6,7) against them. Who do we suppose were 'the Nicolaitans' (Rev. 2: 6,15)? Or who was being described in Jude 8-19 or 2 Peter 2: 12-18? These characteristics are all too evident in what are only human-based organisations.

Christians who have become virtually owned by a sect-like group need to be reminded, *'Actually you are a disciple of one Man only.'*

Q.69

How do we recognise the occult?

I have heard about the Sixth and Seventh Books of Moses. Why are these books not part of the Bible?

True, there is a book that goes under that title – but Moses had nothing to do with it. The so-called Sixth and Seventh Books of Moses are *an occult work* – so named, presumably, because of the extra prestige derived from Moses' name. The last time a copy came my way was when someone who was desperate handed it over to me to be rid of the evil influences that were destroying him. I burnt the book. The Devil's protection is promised to the person who owns it – and who wants that kind of protection?

Christ's coming to this earth has robbed the Devil of his power (Heb. 2:14,15). It is by the **Name** of Christ, the **blood** of Christ, the **Word** of Christ, and by **prayer** in his authority that victory is assured over the world of occult (Latin for *hidden*) things. BUT although the Devil must give way to the power of Christ's death (Col. 2:15) he is still an enemy – active and angry – knowing that his final end is approaching (Rev. 12:12).

Occultism has four main categories.

First, *Superstition* – holding to little taboos – the idea being that an inanimate object can be invested with a force, or even personality.

Secondly, *Fortune-telling* – in about thirty different forms including the use of pendulum, rods, astrology, card reading and horoscopes.

Thirdly, *Magic* – in some fifteen different forms including both black and the supposedly 'white' (healing) magic.

Fourthly, *Spiritism* – or its religious counterpart *Spiritualism* – in some thirty different guises, including table-lifting, levitation, glass-moving, ouija boards, speaking in trance, automatic writing, and clairvoyance.

Although fraud is sometimes part of the deal, these practices are to be firmly avoided – whether experimenting in the school playground or deeper, deliberate involvement.

The Bible is completely hostile to all occult practice (see ch. 16). The reason is that *'the secret* [occult] *things belong to the Lord our God, but the things revealed belong to us and to our children'* (Deut. 29:29). We are to explore all that God *has* revealed to us in his Word, but not the world of the departed and the unseen; they are now in God's domain. *'We are appointed once to die, and then the judgment'*.

When Jesus is proclaimed in places where occultism has been strong, a reaction takes place. The dark powers have to retreat (Acts 19:18,19). Those taken over by evil spirits can be freed through Christ's authority – though only the experienced should undertake this ministry. Christians are safe from these powers provided they do not cross the boundaries.

There is a great difference, then, between magic and prayer. In magic, it is *humans* who are in the driving seat, trying to bend unseen powers to obtain what you want. In prayer it is *God* who is handed the control; our part is prayerfully to place the entire issue before the heavenly Father, leaving the result to *him*.

Q.70

How can I be fulfilled with what I do when I don't want to do it?

A lot of my studies are boring stuff and at times I feel like there is no value in what I do. Is there any purpose to it? How, as a Christian, can I find encouragement?

The apostle Paul would encourage you. *'Whatever you do'*, he declared to the slaves at Colosse, *'work at it with all your heart, as working for the Lord, not for men'* (Col. 3:23).

A slave in the Roman Empire was no more than an **instrumentrum vocale** – 'a tool that can speak'. Yet, for the most part it was the slaves of Rome that provided the raw material for the Gospel to work on. What could provide them with a rationale of work?

1. Work needs a foundation – we find it in Creation

The first 'worker' was God Himself. He satisfied Himself that each stage of Creation was 'good'. The world was a garden, and humans – the summit of God's handiwork – were put into the garden to look after it. Adam's job was to add to his knowledge of everything around him. This is basic. We are custodians, stewards of the Lord, and ultimately it is him that we work and learn for. The Creator gives to work and knowledge its dignity and its normality.

2. Work needs rehabilitation – we find it in Christ

'It is the Lord Christ you are serving' (Col. 3:24). Our human fall is what has adversely affected all that we do: our relationships became soured, our environment is spoilt (Gen. 3: 17,18). The rehabilitation process found its peak in Christ (remember, a carpenter! – and a teacher). With the rise of Christianity, 'knowledge' (a favourite theme among the earlier Greek rationalists) became harnessed to energy and creativity. As Faber's hymn later expressed it:

A servant with this clause makes drudgery divine,
Who sweeps a room, as for thy laws, makes that and the action fine.

The New Testament killed any ideas of a special 'League Table of Work'. Financiers, panel-beaters and computer analysts – it doesn't matter, no category is higher than another. Fellowship provides a wonderful support group at school or in the workplace. Do you join in? The Christian Union, an early breakfast Bible study or the weekly lunchtime meeting? It is good to *remind* each other that our work, our speech, our relationships, are to count for the Lord at what we do!

3. Work needs a model – we see it in the slaves of the Roman empire

Slavery was an evil – but there in the Word of God lay the time bomb, quietly ticking away in the heart of the Roman Empire. Already Christians were learning to ignore difference between slave and master among themselves (Philemon 15 and 16). One day the entire movement would stand over the grave of the Caesars – that's some turnaround!

But Christian slaves were still called upon to do their work well (Titus 2:9). *They* were to be the setting for the bright jewel of the Christian Gospel. Life for them wasn't in the world outside their work. Life was, and is, rising to each new day as a day of adventure with the Lord Jesus Christ – on Planet Earth.

Now, I'm not saying that your teachers are slave owners (though sometimes it might feel that way) but if slaves could find purpose and encouragement in their work then we certainly can.

Q.71

Should Christians use force?

How can people of peace, like Christians, contemplate the use of force?

The violence of the opening years of the twenty-first century has taken our breath away: Terrorist activity and military conflict – the huge loss of life in sieges and wars. These can never be things of which the human race should be proud. The fact that these things cause us distress is not unhealthy – for they can drive us to prayer. It will be helpful to ask some clarifying questions:

1. Do we believe that punishment is right?

The answer, surely, is 'Yes' – if there is such a thing as objective truth (something that is true whatever the circumstances) and a moral code by which human life is ordered. If this were not so, we would have to remove from our vocabulary such words as 'reward', 'merit', 'justice' and even 'forgiveness'.

Punishment is not a popular word in circles that dislike the language of dealing justly with situations that involve wrongdoing. These are people who would rather speak of 'corrective treatment'. However, the apostle Paul is not afraid to speak of the government as 'an avenger who carries out God's wrath on the wrongdoer' (Rom. 13:4 ESV). The treatment of wrongdoing must have an element to it that corrects the wrong.

2. Is there a difference between force and violence?

The use of force is the disciplined exercise of lawful authority – as seen, for example, in the powers of a democratically elected government through a well-regulated police force, a carefully controlled army or a fair system of justice. This is a valid part of God's order. Again, the apostle Paul puts it, 'Let every person be subject to the governing authorities...Whoever resists the authorities resists what God has appointed' (Rom. 13:1,2 ESV).

It seems that 'force' becomes 'violence' when any of these authorities (and others too) act beyond what they are supposed to do if they are acting fairly. Then the ruling authority itself turns to violence. Rev. 13:5-8 portrays all such authorities as a repressive and blasphemous 'beast'. Then you can be justified to call for civil disobedience. The same principle applies when employers become unfair, and strike action is legitimately called for. The earliest Trades Unions themselves were begun through Christian influence.

3. Do we assent to the depravity of the human heart?

This is the teaching that our historic fall into sin (rebellion against God) shows up in every area of our life (Jer. 17:9). The result is that we cannot be trusted and so societies and nations need agreed rules for our order and survival – rules that must be taken seriously. Without such restraints, and the right level of power to apply them, chaos and anarchy result. We can see this happening in the Bible during the leaderless era of the Judges (Judg. 21:25).

The believer should turn away from all forms of violence, but should be committed to the disciplined use of force. A great deal of muddled thinking takes place – especially during times of international conflict – when the debate fails to take account of the difference between violence and force. Force is concerned with the upholding of law. Violence is concerned with the overthrow of law.

Q.72

What is 'the leading of the Spirit'?

I hear a lot of talk about people being 'led by the Spirit'. How, in practical terms, does this happen?

The classic passage is Romans 8 verses 5-17 which shows that the actions of all three Persons of the Trinity are involved in the enabling and 'controlling' of the Christian's life (see especially vv. 9-11). To have the Spirit living in us is the same as having Christ living in us. And, as verse 6 puts it, 'The mind controlled by the Spirit is life and peace' – this points to what John Stott calls *an inner integration*.

When our lives are in harmony with God in this way we don't think or act in a series of uncoordinated or jerky decisions, we think and decide things in a godly way, making decisions and judgements in a manner that 'pleases God' (v.8). In the old Anglican Prayer Book the only prayer request for Whit Sunday is for *a right judgment in all things*. That may not sound as exciting as being led by the Spirit to the right parking spot in a city centre – but it is far more important if we are to get it consistently *right* in the numerous decisions of our complicated lives. There is no greater quality that we could look for in a Christian worker or leader!

You ask how this happens. We are not to be like passive animals that rely on a bit and bridle to be shown where to go (Ps. 32:8,9). Nor have God's purposes anything to do with the 'fatalism' of some eastern belief-systems (see ch. 39). Being 'led' as a Christian is not an endless, hot-line seminar with the Holy Spirit; nor are the details of your wardrobe, meal choices or evening-out plans to be treated as issues that require minute-by-minute guidance from the Holy Spirit.

The maturing believer is not to be like a child, who has to be told at every turn, 'Brush your teeth, put your shoes on, drink your milk!' Spirit-directed Christian living is never infantile (1 Cor. 14:20).

The attitude that should show true, mature decision-making will also be at odds with that of the Sects. Such groups love to possess and control their members, and treat them as having no will of their own. They will require that all finances, even decisions about marriage, should be entrusted to their own authoritarian rule.

We have to learn to recognise that there is a thin dividing line in church life between the 'prophetic' and the 'hysterical' elements. **The place where we transgress the line and become unbalanced is at the point where the Scriptures – of which the Holy Spirit is the author – take second place to the areas of what is sensational and that which 'feels good'.**

Jesus promised that his apostles, exclusively, would be led into all truth (John 16:13). *The New Testament was the fulfilment of this promise.* As our minds are shaped by these Scriptures we can begin to think as the *Spirit* would think – and therefore be led by him.

Q.73

In marriage why must women submit?

I find words like 'submission' and 'obey' very unattractive, in the context of Christian marriage. Surely we've moved on from that?

First a thought, what's motivating you to ask? Is it because you want to find out what the Bible says and obey it, or is it that you are embarrassed to have to defend a different opinion to the culture around you? A key passage is Ephesians 5:21-33. In verse 31 the apostle Paul goes back to the creation principle that lies behind marriage – as Jesus did.

> For this reason a man will leave his father and mother and be united to his wife, and the two will become one flesh (Gen. 2:24).

Your 'unattractive' comment in reality derives from the damage done to marriage as a result of our human fall. Genesis 3:16 sums it up: 'To the woman (the Lord God) said "Your desire will be for your husband, and he will rule over you."'

Here, *desire* is **not** to be seen as an attractive quality. It is the same word as that used in Genesis 4:7 where sin 'desires' to master Cain when he murders Abel. An ugly pattern in marriage, resulting from the Fall, is that of **conflict**. So the passage is talking of a wife with 'desires' of mastery over her husband, and a husband pursuing 'rule' over his wife. The loving, mutually submissive, relationship originally intended degenerates into one of attempted mutual domination. That's where marriage tends to go if we leave it outside the redeeming power of God's good news in Christ.

This, says the New Testament, can be reversed. Wives are to *submit* to their husbands 'as to the Lord' (Eph. 5:22), and husbands are to *love* their wives 'just as Christ loved the church' (v.25). Here is a mutual putting of the other first. 'Submit to one another out of reverence for Christ' (v.21). It means:

Wives submitting and not mastering.

Husbands loving and not ruling.

In both cases this is patterned after *Christ and the relationship he has with his church*. The wife submits to her husband, as head of the wife, as Christ is the head of the church. Christians do not have a problem with submitting to Christ as our Head – because as Saviour *he has loved us* enough to die for us. And husbands should not have a difficulty over doing everything for the benefit of their wives, if they are patterning themselves after Christ who died for the church. To die for their wives? Yes, if necessary – but at the very least putting their wives first in everyday living. The designed result is a 'radiant' (v.27) wife who is fulfilled.

It isn't just Paul. 'Wives', writes Peter, 'in the same way be submissive to your husbands' (1 Peter 3:1). *In the same way*? Peter is referring back to the example of **Christ's submission at the Cross**, 'entrusting himself to him who judges justly'. You see, you can't say that women are inferior if they submit in this way or you would have to say that **Christ was also weak when he submitted on the Cross**. And there was **no inequality**, in submitting his will to that of the Father – both are God. Christ's was a submission of great strength – and so, therefore, is the woman's in marriage at its best.

FOR FURTHER STUDY: Paul Williams on Ephesians 5:21-33, All Souls Audio Cassette Tape Library No. C113/05B (vestry@allsouls.org).

Q.74

Does God allow divorce?

If a marriage ends in divorce – and one of the partners remarries – how far does this take the person out of God's will?

Certainly when Jesus was asked about divorce (Matt. 19:2-9), the assumption would have been that a second marriage had taken place after it. *Is this all right, 'for any and every reason?'* (v.3). There are tensions here that must be taken account of:

1. The tension between the ideal and the actual

The Pharisees would have had Deuteronomy 24:1-4 in mind, as they asked their question. But in Matthew 19:5, Jesus was far more concerned to quote the all-time ideal of *Marriage* in Genesis 2:24. That ideal is always to be our aim while also recognising that, in the Gospel, God meets people at their point of failure – to then lead them on to better things. We can live with this tension, once we understand it.

2. The tension between Law and Contingency (what to do when the law is broken)

There were five different kinds of Law in the Old Testament – the *Creation* laws (relating to the Sabbath and marriage...), the *Covenant* laws (the Ten Commandments), the *Ceremonial* laws that would be fulfilled by Christ's sacrificial death, the *Compassion* laws of the prophets (that emphasised the internal motivation of the heart) – and the **Contingency laws.**

These were the 'What if?' laws, of Deuteronomy, chapters 12–25. Here, marriage is the ideal – *but is there a Plan B if something goes wrong?* Yes, there was. Read Deuteronomy 24:1-4, and notice the frequency of the word 'if' and 'and'. We should also look at the times that Jesus says 'except' – for instance:

except for marital unfaithfulness (Matt. 5:32; 19:9). He is expressing a divine, compassionate accommodation of human weakness. A similar clause is found in 1 Corinthians 7:12.

To the Pharisees, Deuteronomy 24 was a convenient **command** – for separation and divorce. To Jesus, it was a reluctant, yet gracious **concession**. For God ultimately wants to save marriages, not separate them. Christ's first priority for marriage is that it is the great ideal for the church to uphold – it still must be.

3. The tension between Discipline and Grace

Can God forgive, in the face of marital failure? The answer, through the Gospel of grace, is 'Yes'. Otherwise where would King David have been after his sin of 2 Samuel 11? *No one need be written-off.* At the same time the church must, by its teaching and discipline, not allow marriage – which is, after all, how God has designed society to be kept stable – to be weakened by slack practice. *No one else will make this their priority.* This is why churches of every tradition need to have in place the disciplines that help everybody to protect marriage and the family as God intended them to be; yet to do so with the very love of Jesus.

Celsus, the second century pagan critic, flatly disbelieved that the early Christians' upholding of marriage, was possible. 'There', commented the historian T.R. Glover, 'lay the great surprise.' The Christians, he wrote, 'came with a message of the highest conceivable morality... they preached repentance and reformation, and people *did* respond; they repented and lived new lives'.

FOR FURTHER STUDY: *New Issues Facing Christians Today,* John Stott, IVP, chapter 14.

Q.75

What are the rights of an unborn child?

When does an unborn child have the right to live? How does this affect the issue of abortion?

Abortion, and with it, infanticide (the murder of children), was commonplace in the ancient world. Overpopulation or the feared risk of 'a deformed child' would often be the motivation to do away with a child in Greek or Roman society. The general reasoning was that a child only acquired true identity at a period after birth, that its value lies only in its potential usefulness to society, and that only the likelihood of physical wholeness gave it a right to live. *Personhood had to be earned.*

This outlook was in marked contrast to the world of Judaism and the Old Testament law. The true state of the unborn child was highlighted by the Psalmist: -

> For you formed my inward parts; you knitted me together in my mother's womb. I praise you, for I am fearfully and wonderfully made. Wonderful are your works; my soul knows it very well. My frame was not hidden from you, when I was being made in secret, intricately woven in the depths of the earth. Your eyes saw my unformed substance; in your book were written, every one of them, the days that were formed for me, when as yet there were none of them (Ps. 139: 13-16 ESV).

This profoundly affects the very emotional issue of abortion. **At no point of an embryo's existence can the purely biological be separated from the spiritual.** The adult can later reflect, 'At no point was that little blob of protoplasm, anything other than ME.' *There is no moment in the womb of transition from* *animal to human, from non-person to person.* This is common to all of humanity (Job 31:15. See also Jer. 1:5; Isa. 49:5; Luke 1:41-44).

Thus the thinking that characterised early Greek society has to be confronted – a person is always a person in God's eyes – not a non-person that becomes a person. Today the same ideas find expression in the desire to create human embryos for the purpose of research, or providing spare parts. Also to be resisted is any thought of abortion *as a plan, a programme or, as it has become in the West, an industry.*

When in 1967 the British Parliament reformed the abortion law the aim had been to make the law clearer, to outlaw unprincipled abortions and to give legality to doctors who terminated a pregnancy 'in exceptional cases'. The framer of the Parliamentary Bill, David Steel, declared, 'It is not the intention of the promoters of the Bill to leave a wide-open door for abortion on request.' *Yet this very thing has happened.*

Today, concerned people are not powerless to take action. Organisations such as *CARE for the Family* (UK) and *Focus on the Family* (USA) deserve vigorous support, for their provision of education and care. Numerous pregnancy crisis centres exist today, offering counselling, short-term housing and support for those traumatised by the experience of an abortion.

The churches themselves have useful spokesmen. The paediatrics expert, Professor John Wyatt, writes in *Matters of Life and Death* (IVP), '**Nearly always, there is a better alternative to the unwanted or abnormal pregnancy than abortion**'.

Q.76

Is sex only allowed in marriage?

Isn't the church terribly old-fashioned about sex? Is sexual expression really only for those who are married?

Not in ancient pagan circles. Demosthenes wrote, 'We keep prostitutes for pleasure; we keep mistresses for the day-to-day needs of the body; we keep wives for the begetting of children and for the faithful guardianship of our homes.' In Greek society sexual relationships between unmarried people were part of normal living. The same was true for the Roman Empire into which the Christian message crashed at a time of free sex and immoral lifestyles.

William Barclay has written, 'Chastity [restricting sex to marriage] was the completely new virtue which Christianity brought into the world'.

The apostle Paul wrote, 'Avoid sexual immorality, that each of you should learn to control your own body in a way that is holy and honourable' (1 Thess. 4:3). So we are to be *holy* in regard to our relationship towards God, and *honourable* in our relationships towards our neighbours. Paul goes on to write 'not in passionate lust like the heathen, who do not know God'. He is saying that there is a connection between what you know about God and how badly you behave in your morals (see also Rom. 1:18ff).

In Thessalonica, as in all Europe, the established ideas about morality were about to be challenged, then undermined, and finally replaced with a new Christian ethic.

Every generation of Christians has to face this challenge – and it was harder by far for those believers of the first century. *Did we ever expect it would be easy?* We are following the holiest teacher of the purest moral standard in all of history; it is not surprising that the way is hard, revolutionary and against all the trends of the societies around us *in every age*. Genesis 2:24, which is also mentioned later in the Bible by Jesus and Paul, gives us God's norm for how we should deal with our sexual impulses. This amounts to faithfulness in marriage and no sex outside it. That is what our Creator has given us as the right, and the safest, way to channel our human sexual instinct.

The unbelieving world can't take it in. Tertullian of Carthage, in the second century, wrote of the Christians, 'So far from compromising in matters of sex, they are forbidden even a lustful look.' Several false assumptions about sex do need to be challenged though. Try and work on these:

1. Chastity [not having sex] does not mean being unfulfilled. Too often it is assumed that to have not had intimate relationships outside marriage means that you are only half a person. Not so; singleness – as long as it continues to be a Christian's situation – is a charismatic gift, a *charisma* (1 Cor. 7:7).

2. Innocence is not ignorance. It is not those who try to preserve purity who don't know about life – it is promiscuous people who don't even know what life is *for*.

3. Permissiveness is not freedom. As society has become more permissive so it has become less able to deliver real satisfaction and purpose. The widespread use of sex as entertainment, in the same category as putting on a DVD, has not delivered greater human satisfaction or stronger relationships – but quite the opposite.

To speak of the church as needing to 'adapt' to the standards of its time would have been unacceptable to the writers of the New Testament. They expect the standards of the time to change according to the truth they are telling people about!

Q.77

What about desires with people of the same sex?

I am a Christian and am beginning to wonder whether I am of a homosexual orientation. Is there perhaps a church group of people similar to myself that I could join?

I wonder if we can defuse this issue a little? First, let's take out the word 'orientation'. It needs challenging. People talk as though there are only two basic kinds of human being – heterosexuals and homosexuals.

1. There are two categories only of human beings – male and female

The authors of the influential *St Andrew's Day Statement* (ceec@cableinet.co.uk) write that 'At the deepest …level …there is no such thing as 'a' homosexual or 'a' heterosexual; there are human beings, male and female....' This demarcation goes back to the very beginning of things (Gen. 1:27), and we should hold to it. Don't 'label' yourself *a homosexual* – however great the pressure from society.

We can speak of homosexual 'desires' and 'inclinations' – but the theory of a homosexual 'gene' that causes such desires, or the idea that people are born homosexual, have been well exploded. *If homosexuality was genetic*, a pair of identical twins would exhibit the same sexual characteristics but there are plenty of documented cases where one twin will go in a homosexual direction, the other not. What that means is that homosexuality is something that we decide, not something that we are. It is therefore a moral choice.

Peter Tatchell, the well-known British homosexual campaigner says of the 'Gay Gene' theory 'It is totally implausible… is a choice.' Homosexual attractions are generally more likely due to 'an arrested juvenile state' (R.J. Berry, London professor of Genetics). Given time and space, an adolescent will make the transition to a more balanced outlook. *A great many obviously do.*

2. There are two callings only of sexual expression – marriage and singleness

Basic to our understanding of human sexuality are the first two chapters of Genesis. For Genesis 2:24 – endorsed by Jesus and also by the apostle Paul – lays down the all-time divine ideal of a one-man/one-woman lifetime marriage. Christians should hold to this, rejecting *all* extra-marital sexual relationships (which includes homosexual activity).

You will find it a relief if you can hold to this standard because it will spare you the problems of worrying 'should we or shouldn't we?'.

3. There are two responses of the Church – prophetic and pastoral

On the prophetic side it is up to the church to teach and preach on sexuality; and, while we have not always done this effectively, I note that the Anglican World 'Lambeth Conference' of 1998 voted massively against legitimising same-sex unions and the ordaining as clergy anyone involved in same-gender unions.

But, while 'rejecting homosexual practice as incompatible with Scripture', the conference also called for a sensitive and pastoral ministry to people of every sexual disposition.

No, I don't think the call is for you to join a group of others who are aware of homosexual feelings – but rather to be in a group simply of Bible-loving Christian people. Your protection, growth and strength for the future will stem out of ordinary, everyday New Testament fellowship.

FOR FURTHER STUDY: John Stott, *Same Sex Partnerships?* All Souls Audio-tape Library, No. H1/25 (vestry@allsouls.org). www.anglican-mainstream.net is a useful website for reference.

Q.78

Is there such a thing as special prayer for healing?

What is the right place of prayer for healing in public evangelistic meetings? Should we encourage our church members to attend?

When praying for the sick, the best place to do it is in *the local church fellowship*. There we find the best support system – we know each other, we can monitor progress and perhaps learn from our mistakes. We have clear, biblical help for this subject:

> Is any one of you suffering? Let him pray. Is anyone cheerful? Let him sing praise. Is anyone among you sick? Let him call for the elders of the church, and let them pray over him, anointing him with oil in the name of the Lord. And the prayer of faith will save the one who is sick, and the Lord will raise him up (James 5:13-15 ESV).

Note the language. *It is the sick person* who calls for the church leaders to come and pray. This means that no pressure is being put on the sufferer to say that they are healed in order to please the leaders. Then they are to pray 'over' them; the implication is that this is more than a trivial illness; it is something that means that they can't get up!

The oil? This may refer to what was used as medicine in those New Testament days. If this means that medicine and prayer belong together then we are never to reject medical means as a possibility of treatment. We should not think of medicine as being somehow 'unspiritual'. Oil is also symbolic of the Holy Spirit *and* anointing was a biblical way of clearly identifying before the Lord who was the particular focus of prayer.

*The prayer of faith will **save** the one who is sick.* Yes, the Greek word is ambiguous. It can certainly mean that the ill person will be restored physically.

But it can equally refer to spiritual blessings resulting from prayer. It can even imply, if the person dies, a resurrection confidence for the next life. *Whatever the outcome,* 'the Lord will raise him up'. Many times as a church pastor I have said to someone after prayer of this kind 'The Lord will raise you up. It says so!'

It should be made known in the local church that prayer of this kind is available. Learn from Jesus, when he healed it was always personal, you don't read of mass healings in the Gospels. And Jesus needed no platform, no special lights or music and no routine or formula.

It is partly for these reasons that I tend to be wary of big rallies that give advance publicity of healings and miracles as part of the programme. Further, you need to look at the lives of those leading the meetings. **What do they believe? What do they mean by the Gospel? Were they ever involved in clairvoyance or mediumism? How is money handled in their organisation? What about the follow-up and the monitoring of the results?**

Can God heal directly today? Yes, he can but if healing is given it comes as a by-product of the Gospel. It is not the Gospel itself (see ch. 31).

Q.79

How can I learn to pray?

How can I learn to pray? I feel inadequate and ashamed, my thoughts wander and I have no discipline. How can I get off the ground?

You're not alone in your desire. 'Teach us to pray', said Christ's disciples.

No mature Christian that I've ever met has ever taken off their learner plates when it comes to prayer. But let's not stay defeated on the ground, waiting for the ambulance, we have to *just begin*.

Get into the habit as you wake up of greeting the glorious Trinity! Another day of Adventure on Planet Earth with the Lord Jesus Christ! Dedicate that day to God the Father even while your head is still on the pillow. Even before you're out of bed, and as the film of the day in front of you begins to roll on the screen of your mind, ask that the Holy Spirit will fill you *now*, to be a servant of the Lord right through the day. Isn't that worth doing?

Work it out. Obviously time with God is well spent early in the day (see ch. 55). But if your travel demands a very early start, then some other part of the day may be set aside. I don't think that a quiet time on the Metro or on a bus is to be despised at all. I've seen a Muslim doing this with the Koran in London's Euston Station so why not you?

Given this, there is a strong call for Christians to learn the practice of unhurried intercession – that is, praying on our knees on behalf of people, places, churches and world events (1 Tim. 2:1-8). When we do this, we are being 'priests' – acting for God on behalf of others. **We pray; he works.** Intercessory prayer [speaking to God on behalf of others] is God's appointed means by which we may co-operate with the achieving of his will within his world.

Keep it short to begin with and believe that your ability to pray will grow. When prayer is happening an unstoppable power is let loose. We have only to look at the example set by our praying friends where the church is sensationally growing.

Write a list of names and places – keep it on your person. Have different names for each day. 'I pray for you on the nineteenth day of every month' Bishop Alf Stanway of Australia once told me – I was stunned.

But you can do that. **It is possible for intercessors to wield as much influence in countries that they have never been to, as if they were there themselves.** Adopt a country. Get the news about it. Keep newspaper clippings and magazine articles. List the names of those church leaders and mission representatives.

And let's set ourselves targets. 'I used to pray for fifty people a month to become followers of Jesus in my area,' a smiling African leader told me. 'Now I'm praying for a hundred a month!'

FURTHER READING: *Talking about Prayer*, Richard Bewes, Christian Focus Publications.

Q.80

Should I go to the midweek prayer meeting?

Our church is Bible-based and I am there every Sunday but I don't go to the church prayer meeting. Does this matter?

Well, do you want to *really* be Bible-based? If so, I think you will find the will and the means to get to those occasions set up for specific, united prayer. Learn from the apostle Paul:

First of all, then, I urge that supplications, prayers, intercessions and thanksgivings be made for all people, for kings and all who are in high positions, that we may lead a peaceful and quiet life, godly and dignified in every way. This is good, and it is pleasing in the sight of God our Saviour, who desires all people to be saved and to come to the knowledge of the truth. (1 Tim. 2:1-4 ESV)

Here is the priority of prayer in the organising and leading of the church's life. Joint prayer is a key factor in the effective work of the church – as a matter of fact, it *is* the work. Some observations:

1. The praying church is a school of prayer

Prayer in the church is an education. Notice the variety – *supplication [asking for things to happen], prayers, intercessions, thanksgivings.* 'Heaven fights for those who pray' said one Christian preacher. United prayer protects the fellowship, stretches our faith, enriches our experience and widens our view – both upwards to the Lord, and sideways to the farthest horizons.

2. The praying church is a corner-shop of prayer

Do you have an Asian corner-shop in your area? We do and, unlike the out-of-town mega store, you get intimacy, service and the potential to build trust. This should be even truer with the gathering for prayer of Christians who know each other. The result in the community can be what Paul calls 'a peaceful and quiet life'.

The prayer meeting, then, should be central to the life of the church's programme. No one should be elected to eldership in the church unless they understand that they are expected to be at the prayer meeting. No leader or worker should be appointed until they pledge that they will be there. It should also be a priority for the leader or pastor – blocking the date off right through the year.

3. The praying church is a web-site of prayer
The slogan ought to be *our church could touch the world.* Have you noticed the universal scope of prayer in the passage? *For all people... kings.. .all those in high positions... desire all people to be saved.*

No church should aim to be a mega church but every fellowship should aspire to be **a world church** – with threads of influence and power leading out from it everywhere. 'It is prayer, and prayer alone', wrote Jacques Ellul, 'that can make history'.

Shouldn't you be part of that if you call yourself a Christian?

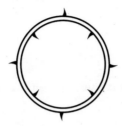

PART FIVE
THE CHRIST WE FOLLOW

When a portrait is spoiled, the only way to renew it is for the subject to come back to the studio and sit for the artist all over again. That is why Christ came – to make it possible for the divine image in man to be re-created.

We were made in God's likeness; we are re-made in the likeness of his Son.

Athanasius of Alexandria,
AD296-373: translation from *After the Gospels,* David Winter, Mowbrays, London

Q.81

Is Jesus the only one to follow?

How can I be confident that Jesus is the ultimate figure in all history for us to follow?

The human race is haunted by Jesus Christ. Films, books and articles about him are everywhere. Often they present a very distorted view but it is *him*, rather than other religious leaders, that the debate is about. Previous 'deities' that were huge in their time have all in turn been obliterated by this one great name.

Even figures of history, associated only for a short time with Christ, have become universally famous. We would never have heard of Pontius Pilate except for that one meeting with Jesus that made Pilate's one of the top 10 best-known names in all history; *'He was crucified under Pontius Pilate'* is declared worldwide in many churches every Sunday.

Children everywhere have been named after Christ's disciples. 'In years to come,' wrote Andrew Knowles, 'people would call their dogs "Caesar" and their sons "Matthew"; just one of the changes Jesus makes!' (*The Way Out*, Collins).

But take it further still, here are some pointers:

1. Christ's unique character

Few will say that Jesus was anything other than supremely good (see chapter 61). His goodness was endorsed by *his friends* (1 Peter 2:22) who had every opportunity to see him at close range; also by *his enemies* who could not make a single charge against him stick. Most remarkably of all *he himself* makes the claim that he had not committed, nor had any, sin (John 8:46). This was unlike all other spiritual leaders who, as they advanced in character, become increasingly aware of their own moral imperfection.

2. Christ's unique conduct

Let me list only a few. *Christ forgave people their sins* – even the sins that they had committed against individuals whom Jesus had never met. This provoked the charge of blasphemy for 'Who can forgive sins but God alone?' (Mark 2:5-7). Further *Jesus accepted the worship of people* (John 20:28). True, there are 'gurus' today who receive worship but they invariably end up in a tomb. *Jesus rose from the dead.*

3. Christ's unique claims

Jesus made numerous claims including that he was *the Son of God* in a special and unique sense (John 1:18). His relationship to 'the Father' was such that he would refer to 'my Father and your Father' (John 20:17); never to 'our Father' – except in the case of the Lord's Prayer when he was teaching us what **we** should pray. Jesus also did not hesitate to use the divine name 'I AM' of himself (John 8:58).

Further, Jesus claimed to be the *Universal Judge* (Matt. 7:22, 23; John 5: 22, 23). No one else ever claimed the right to decide upon the eternal destiny of all people. Lastly, Christ claimed to be the *Centre of all truth,* drawing all people to himself (John 12:32, 46; 14:6).

Either Jesus was what he claimed to be, or he was not. No one who was *wrong* on such massive issues could possibly be 'mistaken', he would have to be mad. But madness has never been attributed to Jesus.

FOR FURTHER STUDY: *Thinking Clearly about the Uniqueness of Jesus,* Chris Wright, Monarch Publications.

Q.82

Who is the real Christ?

Books, plays, paintings and even preachers have got me somewhat confused as to what Jesus is really like. What is he on about? What is his game plan?

This question was asked by an enquirer in the *Christianity Explored* course at All Souls Church in London. Certainly a whole galaxy of 'Christ' figures tend to be paraded by groups and organisations anxious to attract people to their programmes – to suit *their* own 'game plan'.

People have been doing this ever since Christ's first hearers tried to turn him into a liberator from the Roman occupation. Even Herod, at the time of Jesus' trial, hoped that the prisoner might turn entertainer (Luke 23:6-8).

And so, across the centuries, we have been misled by the *Military Christ* of the Crusades and, in contrast, by the *Sentimental Christ* of English Victorian gentility. The Christ who has been called upon to bless battleships in one generation can be invoked to bless guerrilla fighters in the next. In our own time we have been faced by the claims of Jesus the *Political Messiah*; alternatively by those of a *Social Justice Christ*. Show-business people have interpreted Jesus as a *Superstar Christ*; religious existentialists [those who only believe in what they can sense] as a *Signs and Wonders* miracle worker.

Through the ages there has been an *Artists' Christ*; he has been painted youthful and virile, pale and emaciated, severe and majestic, other-worldy and remote. There is a *feminine* version of Christ, or the Ché Guevara-like image of *the revolutionary*. Jesus has, in turn, been *a clown, a dancer, a radical, a tramp*. It is the way of what is called Postmodernism, to encourage the creation of your own *Designer Christ*, who can be cut and pasted to fit your particular programme.

Perhaps it is around the word *programme* that we can establish an answer to the question. On the whole, those who wish to adopt a Christ of their own making have defined him by what he can 'do' for their chosen cause.

Who is he? What did he come for? When we consult the primary documents that tell us of Jesus Christ we are forced to conclude that he has his own programme – preset and ordained from eternity – for he is '**the Lamb that was slain from the creation of the world**' (Rev. 13:8). The answer lies precisely there (see also chapter 27).

The *programme* for his representatives and agents, then, is made very clear by the apostle Paul:

> I decided to know nothing among you except Jesus Christ and him crucified (1 Cor. 2:2).

How authentic your Christ is stands or falls by the test of the Cross. In Jesus' own words, 'The Son of Man came not to be served, but to serve, and to give his life as a ransom for many' (Mark 10:45). If your 'Christ' did not come to die for the sins of the world, and to bear their penalty, you had better change your Christ at once.

FOR FURTHER STUDY: *Christianity Explored – an Enquirers' course*: www. christianityexplored.com

Q.83

How can the truth be found in just one man?

I struggle to understand how in one man, Jesus, we can know God and the truth about all of life. Can you help?

Read John's Gospel. Just to read it has helped millions. By the time the reader arrives at chapter 5 the conviction is growing '*This man is God: he knows everything*'.

'Logic is the Logos', wrote Athanasius of the fourth century AD. He was referring to John 1:1-14, where Christ is identified as *The Word* (Greek: '*Logos*'). By 'Logic', Athanasius meant the methodology, the rationale, **the explanation** of something. If, for example, you understand 'the logos' of meteorology, or of biology, then you understand its nature, its purpose and direction.

As far as life is concerned, Jesus is both its goal and starting point (see chs. 1 and 24). Athanasius helped the church to understand this truth more fully during the controversies that boiled up around the nature of Christ's person. As he put it: **Only Jesus, as God, can reveal God.**

The *English Standard Version* of the Bible is helpful in its translation of John 1:18: 'No one has ever seen God; the only God, who is at the Father's side, he has made him known.' This 'Revealer' – who is the same as God – is, of course, Jesus. Matthew 11:27 gives us the same truth from the words of Christ himself.

In the face of false teachers, such as Arius (who maintained that Christ was 'similar to' God, but not 'the same as' God), Athanasius was adamant; his faithfulness to Scripture was rewarded at last in the Council of Nicea in AD325*. Its statement has become part of the historic church creed. There it is said of Christ that he is ...*God of God, Light of Light, Very God of very God, Begotten, not made, Being of one substance* (the vital word) *with the Father...*

Some people ask, 'Can the **Son** of God be truly God?' Yes, this is our understanding of the Trinity (ch. 22). Christ is of the same *substance,* or nature, as the Father. It was with all due reverence that the evangelist Vijay Menon once colourfully illustrated it, 'The son of a tiger is a tiger; the son of a baboon is a baboon; the Son of God...is *God*'.

There is unanimity in the New Testament on this truth. The term 'The Lord' (Greek: *kurios*) is used fourteen times of **God** in the opening chapter of Luke's Gospel. Then, in the rest of the Gospel the same word is used fourteen times of **Jesus Christ**. The implication is obvious; *Jesus is God.*

> He (Christ) is the radiance of the glory of God and the exact imprint of his nature (Heb. 1:3 ESV).

In all the Letters of the New Testament, Christ is referred to only 22 times by his human name, Jesus, but 701 times by some form of expression that acknowledges his deity.

Jesus is fully God and fully man. 'It followed', wrote Athanasius, 'that he alone was able to recreate everything and to be an ambassador for all men with the Father.'

* Dan Brown, in the Da Vinci Code, says that before this the church didn't think of Jesus as being God. You only have to read some of the references above to see that this is not true. It's rather like saying that gravity did not exist before Isaac Newton 'discovered' it!

Q.84

Why did Jesus have a virgin birth?

I can't see why the virgin birth of Jesus is important. Please explain.

The virgin birth of Jesus is taught in the Scriptures and is reinforced in all the historic Christian creeds. **It has nothing to do with any supposed Christian belief that human sexual relationships were in themselves sinful and were therefore inappropriate to the birth of the Son of God.**

You can also forget all notions, common in pagan literature, of deities having sexual relations with humans. What the Bible account reverently presents is the combination of Christ's **manward** side (the human name *Jesus* and his human birth) and his **Godward** side (the title *Son of God* and his supernatural conception).

Both Gospels of Matthew and Luke, independently of each other, feature infancy stories of Jesus. Both are in clear agreement that the conception of the child was not caused by the involvement of an earthly father but rather through the direct, supernatural intervention of the Holy Spirit. In Matthew 1:23, the Old Testament prophecy of Isaiah 7:14 is quoted, **'Behold, the virgin shall conceive and bear a son, and they shall call his name Immanuel'**. (Virgin, Greek *'parthenos'*, represents a word in the Hebrew text that means a 'young woman' that at the time, and in the context, implied a pure, unmarried woman.)

Mark's Gospel has no cause to mention the virgin birth – for it begins not with the birth of Jesus but with his public ministry. The Gospel of John begins on a different level altogether, developing further the profound truth of the Incarnation [Jesus coming from heaven to take human form].

It is really the virgin *conception* of Jesus that was miraculous; the *birth* was like that of any baby. The key passage for our understanding, for which the *English Standard Version* provides the best translation, runs as follows:

And Mary said to the angel, 'How will this be, since I am a virgin?' And the angel answered her, 'The Holy Spirit will come upon you, and the power of the Most High will overshadow you; therefore the child to be born will be called holy – the Son of God' (Luke 1:34,35 ESV).

Therefore the obvious conclusion to be drawn from the angel's words is that the birth of **a truly holy human being** was the chief outcome of this miraculous event. The virgin birth is not, in itself, a proof of Christ's deity; even Muslims believe in the virgin birth. Nor did Jesus *become* Son of God at his conception and birth; he has always been the Son. Rather, we have in this teaching the God-given indication that *Jesus was not affected by the sinfulness that is part of all human beings' nature since the fall.*

Consequently, Jesus – though God incarnate – grew and developed as a normal human being (Luke 2:40,50,51). Yet despite experiencing human temptations as we do, he did not sin (Heb. 4:15; 7:26). This means that he is the only human being who can credibly stand for us, speak for us and suffer for our sins. A sinful person's sacrifice would not be effective as **who would then pay for their sins?**

Q.85

Did Jesus really physically come back from the dead?

Must we be held to the crudeness of a literal resurrection of Jesus Christ? Is it not enough to describe the Easter event as a wonderful metaphor of the Christian hope?

There are some books written by 'academics' that solemnly put forward theories like this but we only need ten minutes thought to realise that we are in dreamland if we think like that. *Just think!*

Here are twelve men whose world has come to an end. One of them has already committed suicide (Judas Iscariot); another has publicly denied that he had ever met Jesus and is now a broken man; yet another takes the mother of the crucified leader into his own home. It looks like an obvious end-of-story sequel. Just to round things off the pessimist in the group had forecast disaster all along (John 11:16).

One arrest in the garden of Gethsemane and the twelve disintegrate completely (Matt. 26:56). Given that, what caused them ever to come together again – to the extent that their enemies would later describe them as 'men who have turned the world upside down' (Acts 17:6 ESV)? **All this as a result of a metaphor? Please!**

As well as the changed lives of the disciples there is an empty tomb to be explained. We hear from time to time of someone who has managed to come back from a death (or near-death) experience – some even having been nailed down in the coffin first! – **but how long does the excitement last?** I can just remember such an event, a man had 'died' and then made the come-back. The news item just squeezed into the BBC *World at One* news programme. I never saw it featured in any paper. What was the man's name? – I'd forgotten it within ten minutes. One day, though, it *will* appear on a gravestone somewhere.

If Jesus Christ had not clearly – and indisputably – been physically raised from the dead as the permanent conqueror of death on behalf of the human race, we would never have heard of him. The demoralised movement would have fizzled out on the launching pad. For a while, memories of a carpenter-healer would have persisted around Galilee; then 'The Jesus Event' would have ended up like *The Theudas Event* (Acts 5:36), washed over like a child's sandcastle on the beach by the tides of history.

Look at 1 Corinthians 15:3-5, where, **in a single, unbroken sentence,** Christ is the subject of four verbs; He died, was buried, was raised, and appeared. Implication: **what was raised was what was buried.**

Do the metaphor theorists think Jesus actually died? **Yes, yes.** Was buried? **Sure.** Was raised on the third day? (always that insistence on 'the third day'!) **Er, no – that's metaphorical.** Appeared? **No, that's metaphorical too.**

So within a single sentence, Paul can switch from factual language to metaphorical language? **Please!....**

FURTHER READING: *The Resurrection: Fact or Fiction?* Richard Bewes, Lion Publishing. See also chapter 50.

Q.86

What evidence is there for the Ascension?

I have been challenged by a critic that there is no evidence among the Gospel writers that Jesus ascended to heaven; that Mark 16:19 is not part of the original Greek text, and that Luke 24:51 is not supported by the best early manuscripts. How valid is this criticism?

You are referring to the phrase that Jesus 'was carried up into heaven'. Certainly Mark 16:9-20 comes within the category of a footnote rather than the main Gospel text (see ch. 48). But although not *all* the early Greek manuscripts of Luke 24:51 include the phrase *and was carried up into heaven,* 'it is found in manuscripts and versions of the highest character, and ought certainly to be retained' (W.B. Jones DD, *The Speaker's Commentary,* 1878*).* Supporting documents include the major 'Alexandrinus' and 'Vaticanus' manuscripts (see ch. 41).

Actually, if your questioner had read more widely, he would have learnt that Christ's Ascension is a theme running through the Scriptures. It is not limited to just these two sections above.

1. The Ascension of Jesus is consistent with the ancient prophecies
Psalm 68:18, which refers to 'God' ascending on high and 'leading captives in his train', is quoted in the New Testament and directly connected with the Ascension of Jesus (Eph. 4:7-10). Other references include Psalms 47:5; 110:1.

2. The Ascension of Jesus is recognised as the goal of the Gospel story
Your friend evidently missed other instances of the phrase in question: 'As the time approached for him *to be taken up to heaven.*' (Luke 9:51). The Ascension is seen here as the end goal of Christ's journey, the triumphant celebration of his saving work at the Cross.

3. The Ascension of Jesus was directly announced by himself

The risen Jesus told Mary Magdalene, "Do not cling to me, for *I have not yet ascended* to the Father; but go to my brothers and say to them, "*I am ascending* to my Father and your Father, to my God and your God"' (John 20:17 ESV). It couldn't be clearer.

4. The Ascension of Jesus was directly reported by the Gospel writers

Luke 24:51 has already been referred to. In his sequel to his gospel, the Acts of the Apostles, Luke declares that his Gospel took the reader through the story of Jesus '*until the day when he was taken up...*' (Acts 1:2). Luke now goes on to relate how '....*he was lifted up* and a cloud took him out of their sight, (Acts 1:9). Clear enough?

5. The Ascension of Jesus is interpreted in the light of his return

Luke again 'And while they were gazing into heaven as he went, behold, two men stood by them in white robes and said, "Men of Galilee, why do you stand looking into heaven? This Jesus *who was taken up from you into heaven* will come in the same way as you saw him go into heaven"' (Acts 1:10,11 ESV).

It just goes to show you that you have to do your research rather than just take someone's opinion at face value – so let's get these, and other references, into our heads (John 6:62; 16:28; Acts 3:21 ESV; Eph. 1:20-22). We want to help ourselves, and our friends, to know about the ascended triumph of our Lord.

Q.87

What is Jesus doing in Heaven?

What is meant by the idea of Jesus praying, or interceding, for us in heaven? Why does he need to do that?

Some have mistakenly thought that our Lord is somehow 're-offering' the sacrifice of his death before the Father in heaven, and in so doing is 'pleading' on our behalf. It is even claimed in some circles that this happens during the service of Holy Communion – that, in a special way, the Cross of Calvary is being *freshly presented* in heaven at that moment for the forgiveness of our sins.

But that would be to deny the 'once-for-all' nature of what took place when Jesus died for the sins of the world at a certain time and place in history. At the Transfiguration, Moses and Elijah were seen speaking with Jesus about the 'departure' (literally 'exodus') that Jesus would accomplish for the sins of the world when he died. We read that this was not to take place in heaven *but on earth at Jerusalem* (Luke 9:30, 31). The New Testament is clear in its insistence that Christ's death was historically once and for all achieved and never to be repeated – or re-offered:

> 'He is able to save to the uttermost those who draw near to God through him, since he always lives to make intercession for them ...He has no need, like those high priests, to offer sacrifices daily, first for his own sins, and then for those of the people, since he did this once for all when he offered up himself.' (Heb. 7: 25, 27 ESV)

It is already done. Only when we have understood that a way into the Father's presence has been fully and finally secured can we really take in the wonder of the atonement [Jesus paying the penalty of sin] and of Christ's present ministry on behalf of his followers. His work that he came to do on earth is finished. What, then, is he doing now in heaven?

The Christian is assured that the goodness of Christ's unrepeatable, sacrificial death means that he is now in heaven as Man (not an 'ex-man') **to represent us before the Father** (1 John 2:1). It is in *that* sense that he may be said to be 'pleading' for us.

No, this is not a continuous (or repeated) *re-offering* of the sacrifice of the Cross; that would be to undercut the certainty and finality of our redemption. Nor is Christ's 'intercession' a continuous stream of uttered petitions.

The thrilling truth is that Jesus Christ is ever-living in heaven *to support our case, to guarantee our complete forgiveness and to escort us into the Father's presence every time we turn to God's throne in prayer.* Any time I desire to approach the Father, Christ is there at the Father's side – as the one who died for me to ensure that I get a hearing! There is a Man in heaven, a perfect Man, our Intercessor. That is why Christian prayer ends with 'In Jesus Christ's Name'. He is our *only* way through.

Q.88

Is having the Holy Spirit an 'extra' to having Jesus?

What was happening at Pentecost? Is this an extra dimension on top of following Jesus and being born again?

Not exactly. Christ earlier promised us that if we believed then we would be born again and have the Holy Spirit living and working inside us. Pentecost is the *fulfilment* of this on an international scale. Luke's Gospel ends with Jesus pledging, 'I am going to send you what my Father has promised' (Luke 24:49). Luke's book of Acts was to be the exhilarating sequel of the Holy Spirit's work.

Supposing the book of Acts had been lost? We would have found it almost impossible to explain the phenomenal power and boldness of the early Christians. The book opens with the historic gathering of Pentecost; with the sound of the rushing mighty wind; with flames of fire that settled on the disciples and the miracle with which the amazed listeners heard the Gospel being announced to them (each in their own language Acts 2:1-13). Pentecost gave the Gospel of the New Birth an international platform! It was a *unique* event, a *universal* event and a *saving* event.

All this had been prophesied in the Old Testament – as Jesus explained when teaching Nicodemus about the New Birth (see ch. 28). He had taught his disciples that the Holy Spirit, 'another counsellor', would come and live within them (John 14:16-18). Not a *different* counsellor but (as the New Testament Greek implies) a *second* Counsellor or 'Helper' (ESV) who would be the 'other' unseen presence of Jesus himself – accessible to believers in China, the Americas, Africa or anywhere.

An illustration may be helpful. Picture a famous musician coming down the aeroplane gangway at Seoul Airport. A thousand fans are eagerly waiting just for a glimpse – maybe four or five might even get an autograph? However, the contact can only be disappointingly limited, after a few minutes the celebrity steps into a car and is driven away but later that evening comes the explanation. There on the screen, in the TV concert, is the same familiar person – now made accessible to millions of fans, by another medium.

Christ was taken away from the few in order to become accessible to the many – to believers on every continent. Through 'another Counsellor' (the third Person of the Trinity), the very presence of Christ himself is not only brought into your home but, even better, is brought right into your heart and life.

When we have been born again, we sense that 'Christ has come into my life'. That is true. *Christ* has become real to us – as our Lord and ever-present companion. However, technically speaking, it is the Holy Spirit who, as Christ's 'other self', has taken up residence within us.

It is because the Spirit always draws attention to *Christ* (John 16:14) that he doesn't put himself forward. A Spirit-filled person is a Christ-centred and Christ-aware person (see ch. 33). The Spirit is the 'Executive' of the Godhead. **He puts us to work, to accomplish IN us all that Jesus came to do FOR us at the Cross.** He makes forgiveness and the Lord's friendship a personal reality, for all of our days.

Q.89

How is Christ coming back?

Isn't the idea of Jesus of Nazareth physically returning to earth a bit quaint to believe in our connected world of e-mails and the Internet?

Not if we have studied the Bible. Many people today have an incredibly feeble conception of the future; it is vague and wishy-washy. It usually follows that the present won't make much sense for them at all either. It is only when you can see where the world and history are heading, that the present – your own present – is lit up with meaning and purpose.

The coming of the Lord Jesus Christ will take place personally, powerfully, physically, visibly, publicly – and *instantly*. Read Matthew 24:30, 31, or 1 Thessalonians 4:13–5:3. It will be quicker than any e-mail. Here are words of Jesus:

> For as the lightning flashes and lights up the sky from one side to the other, so will the Son of Man be in his day (Luke 17:24).

This will be no local happening ('Look there!' or 'Look here!' – Luke 17:23). That day, the world won't be seeing a carpenter from Nazareth wearing Galilean homespun. It will be Jesus in his incandescent brilliance as the 'Son of Man', as foreseen by Daniel back in the Old Testament (Dan. 7:13,14). Centuries later, Peter, James and John were to witness their familiar Master 'transfigured', as the same irradiated Person – a dramatic preview of Christ's triumphant final rule (Luke 9:28-36).

Stephen, the martyr, as he was about to die had a similar glimpse: 'Behold I see the heavens opened, and the Son of Man standing at the right hand of God' (Acts 7:56). The exiled apostle John on the island of Patmos saw the same figure: *'his face was like the sun shining in full strength'* (Rev. 1:16). The whole world will finally witness this same spectacle (Rev. 1:7).

The return of Christ will mark the end of history as we know it. It will bring on the final Judgment. It will re-unite the Lord with his church on earth. It will bring about the new heaven and the new earth. Pain, death, persecution, poverty and sorrow will all be banished. The entire edifice of evil that has raised itself against the rule of God will be taken to pieces in a moment.

> One day great Babylon will tell its ashen story,
> Drunk with her worldly power, her sins piled to the sky;
> Standing astride her grave, the martyred saints in glory
> Sing their hallelujahs as the smoke goes up on high.
> (R.T. Bewes, Jubilate Hymns: jubilateMW@aol.com)

We have been warned all along not to place a date or a time upon the Second Coming of Christ (Matt. 24:42-44). Many people ignore this warning and waste endless hours trying to work it out. The way in which we should be spending our days before the end is to work, watch and witness – whether or not yours is a world of computers, e-mail and all the rest!

FOR FURTHER STUDY: *The Vision of His Glory*, Anne Graham Lotz, Word Publishing; *The Lamb Wins*, Richard Bewes, Christian Focus Publications.

Q.90

Is it OK to go to other religious events?

Is it wrong to hold multi-religious services? After all, would it not be helpful to combine the best of all the world's beliefs?

Our attitude towards those of other belief-systems must be one of firmness, combined with courtesy and grace. It is good to get to know people of other beliefs and at times to engage in discussion and open debate. It is not impossible for Christian believers to attend an event organised by people of another religion – provided it's understood that you are looking on, rather than taking part.

But we still have to remember that those who reject Jesus's claims on their life are outside his covenant, and so are lost people. They desperately need the good news of his saving death for the sins of the world *and no one is beyond the reach of his voice* (see ch. 37).

Once you let people think that faith in Christ is just one of many possible alternatives you deny the principle for which first-century Christians were thrown into the arena or burnt to death. In the days of the Roman Empire they were killed not because they believed that Jesus was divine (the political authorities allowed for as many gods as you liked!) but because they insisted that Jesus was the *only* Lord. He was to be worshipped exclusively, different from any contending saviour, messiah, or Caesar-god. They refused to accept a place for Christ as one alongside other 'gods' – part of the Roman *Pantheon*. If you team up with another religion you are saying, 'As a Christian, I am wrong'.

The prophet Elijah had to combat a similar mindset, when confronted by the prophets of Baal (1 Kings 18). People must have argued with Elijah, 'These Baal-worshippers are really pretty decent people, you know. They aren't all that different from us. It would be an *enrichment* working with them.' Elijah wouldn't have it and the result was the preservation of God's unique revelation so that Jesus could come so that we would know the Gospel today.

The Bible presents a single, undivided proposal of the only true God. A God *who is defined as the God and Father of our Lord Jesus Christ* (see chapters 1 and 24). It is meaningless to talk in vague terms of 'God' as something/someone out there – as though that title can incorporate every contrasting and contradictory belief in sight. When talking to people of other faiths politely challenge them to 'Please describe your relationship to the Jesus Christ of space, time and history.'

You still want a synthesis of beliefs? To reconcile every best principle and tradition in a single system? Our answer is, '**It's been done already**'. The New Testament tells us this about Christ – 'In him all the fullness of God was pleased to dwell, *and through him to reconcile to himself all things, whether on earth or in heaven, making peace by the blood of his cross.*'

One Man has done it. And he is big enough to hold the world together.

Q.91

Am I a real disciple of Jesus?

How can I be sure that my faith is genuine, and that it won't turn out to be bogus?

We are encouraged to look at ourselves to 'make your calling and election sure' (2 Peter 1:10). Here is a helpful summary using all three persons of the Trinity as a foundation – not in a smug or arrogant way but in an assured and humble way. It will help you know if you have trusted Christ for salvation and whether you are a true believer.

1. The Word of God to us
I rely for my beliefs on God's unchanging Word, not on my inner changeable feelings. Christ comes and knocks at the door of my life (Rev. 3:20), I respond to his dying love for me and, in thankful trust, invite him in. **Ask yourself, did he come in?**

You may reply 'Er...well, I hope so! Um...but I don't *feel* that he has come in!'

But look again; it's a **promise**: 'If anyone hears my voice and opens the door, I **will** come in.' So, did he come in? *Why, he must have done, because it says so!*

It is good to memorise other great statements of assurance such as John 1:12; 5:24; 6:37; Romans 8:1; 1 John 5:11-13. Naturally, there is no room for becoming slack about our moral *state* but as for *where we stand* – our position in God's eyes – God does not want us to remain in doubt. *He has already transferred the believer into the kingdom of his Son* (Col. 1:13,14). It says so!

2. The work of Christ for us
The Bible teaches us that, at the Cross, the lifting of our guilt was *done*, so that we could be set free from the anger of the coming judgment. That we could be fully accepted by God here and now (Rom. 5:6-9).

We do need *reminders* of this (for example, the service of Holy Communion – see chapter 36) but to imagine that *we* could somehow add our own efforts to secure our salvation would be to insult Christ in his dying love for us. So test yourself: *Is it the death of Jesus that I am relying upon for my eternal salvation?* He has died for me as a once and for all saving event. I don't have to do anything more, I can't do anything more – except believe.

3. The witness of the Spirit in us

'The Spirit himself bears witness with our spirit that we are children of God' (Rom. 8:16). The Spirit does *in* us what Christ did *for* us, making Christ and his blessings real and personal (see ch. 88). Inwardly he confirms our position as we begin to recognise that he really is working in us – in terms of a changed, and changing, life.

The authentic believer is only too aware of the power that sin still has in our lives (Rom. 7:24) *but we do know where the answer to that problem lies.* Learn the three 'tenses' of Salvation (end of chapter 30) and take in the words of John Newton, the converted slave trader, 'I am not what I ought to be; I am not what I wish to be; I am not what I hope to be; *but by the grace of God I am not what I was!*'

FUTHER STUDY: *Beginning the Christian Life*, Richard Bewes, Christian Focus Publications.

Q.92

Can I lose my salvation?

Aren't there indications in the Bible that believers can lose their salvation? – Like Hebrews chapter 6.

Well, it does look that way at first:

> For it is impossible to restore again to repentance those who have once been enlightened, who have tasted the heavenly gift, and have shared in the Holy Spirit, and have tasted the goodness of the word of God and the power of the age to come, if they then fall away, since they are crucifying once again the Son of God to their own harm and holding him up to contempt (Heb. 6:4-6 ESV).

But a look at the context of this passage brings out the meaning. These were *Hebrew* members of the Christian church. The 'foundation' (vv.1,2) had already been laid for them in Old Testament Judaism: 'repentance', 'faith in God', 'washings', the 'laying on of hands', the doctrine of the 'resurrection' and 'eternal judgment'. *All of these were a valid part of Jewish teaching and practice.*

The problem for these worshippers was that, because of the similarity between some of the 'foundational' Old Covenant practices and those of the New Covenant in Christ, they were easily tempted to go back to what they knew of before. *It was as if they had never really trusted in Jesus from the start.* This is why it is no good to 'once again' lay the foundation of the Old Testament; you can't lay a foundation twice. They *must* leave these elementary Old Testament doctrines of Christ and move on to 'maturity' (v.1), the full experience of life in Christ, if they are to have any hope.

None of the language here is that of Justification or the New Birth. If they had only been enlightened but not saved (justified); if they had only tasted and shared but not been transformed (born again); then, humanly speaking, it would be 'impossible' to win them over again. By now they were 'inoculated' against the real thing.

It can happen today when someone who believes in God in a general way apparently becomes a Christian – *it looks like a conversion.* When they go back to what they were like before people wonder how they could have 'fallen away'. The more likely truth is that whilst you were worshipping God *they had never actually ceased worshipping their old deity.* The whole thing was fake from start to finish.

Lapsed cynics will sometimes say, 'I tried Christianity once but it didn't work for me.' Were they ever really saved? Not if they stay in their non-believing state.

'They went out from us, but they were not of us; for if they had been of us, they would have continued with us. But they went out, that it might become plain that they all are not of us' (1 John 2:19 ESV).

On a more positive note, it really seems that 'Once saved, we are always saved' (see ch. 91). Please look up John 6:37; 10:28,29; Hebrews 13:5 and plenty more. Can a believer be lost? *No – but don't try to test the idea.*

Q.93

I want to be holy – but I know I'm not !

Why am I not more effective in making a success of my life as a Christian? I sometimes despair over my slow rate of moral progress. I just can't seem to escape from what I used to be like.

To answer this we need to know the difference between **Justification** (see ch. 29) and **Sanctification**. Many people never get this sorted.

Associated with 'sanctification' are words like 'saint', 'separation' and 'holy'. A *saint*, in New Testament terms is simply someone who has been 'set apart', or separated for God and for holiness. So, although Christians may often think of themselves as 'sinners', the New Testament never treats them as anything other than 'saints'. See how the apostle Paul addresses even the unruly church at Corinth:

> To the church of God that is at Corinth, to those sanctified in Christ Jesus, called to be saints...(1 Cor. 1:2)

There are two ideas within the idea of sanctification.
First, as a result of God working in us, we are 'in Christ'. We are set aside for God and his service. This happens as part of Christian conversion. This is *positional sanctification* – it is instantaneous with justification. We may not feel like saints, but we **are** saints, from Day One.

Second, there is what may be called *conditional sanctification*. Those Corinthian believers mentioned above were not only already 'sanctified' in Christ but they were also called to *be* saints and to *become* holy. This is a process that depends on us changing using the grace God gives us – the Bible, prayer, Church fellowship and the sacraments. On the whole it is this *process* that we normally think of as sanctification.

Justification, then, is instantaneous – like the taking of a photograph. Sanctification is more like the processing of the film. Steadily, progressively, **we become more like Jesus in character.** Justification is when righteousness is *imputed* (credited, given) to a person. It's like a player being transferred to a new soccer team. That team's facilities, identity and reputation is given to you. Sanctification is when righteousness is *imparted* – like starting to play for the new team and using the facilities to develop your skills to play in it. It is by the power of God's Spirit, living within us, that we grow in faith and obedience. My colleague Rupert Higgins has said that it's the difference between getting married, *a fact*, and becoming a good husband or wife, *a process.*

So it is never going to be quick. No one is going to wake up one morning and declare, 'Well, I never; I've become holy!' **In fact, the sure-fire sign of the new birth in Christians is that they are aware of their sins and long to overcome them.** Take a look at Paul's words as an advanced believer (Rom. 7:24,25) and take comfort from them! Awareness of sin is a healthy sign that we have turned around and are now swimming *against* the current. If you were still swimming downstream you wouldn't feel the force of the water trying to drag you back.

The power of the sin that still troubles you, then, is not going to be got rid of, or eradicated, by the Spirit's working. It is going to be opposed or *counteracted.* We will be battling for holiness all our days.

Here is a fine apostolic prayer to help you:

> Now may the God of peace himself sanctify you completely, and may your whole spirit and soul and body be kept blameless at the coming of our Lord Jesus Christ. He who calls you is faithful; he will surely do it (1 Thess. 5:23,24).

Q.94

What should I do when I'm tempted?

I hear people speak about the power we are given to overcome our sins but what, practically, should I do when I face the Devil's pressures?

A little girl was asked in her Bible class what she did when she was tempted. 'Well,' she replied, 'I send Jesus to the door.'

At that level it was a very creditable reply but it's really Christ who sends *us* to the door. Following Christ is not a **passive** affair, you don't just sit back and let Jesus do it all for you. Notice that in the New Testament the verbs about overcoming temptation are **active.** You get words like 'wrestle' (Eph. 6:12), 'fight' (1 Tim. 6:12), 'resist' (1 Peter 5:9), 'run' (Heb. 12:1), 'flee' (2 Tim. 2:22).

The old Church of England Prayer Book says that we are to 'beat down Satan under our feet'.

Before Christ's Spirit entered our life we couldn't really do battle at all – we were like prisoners. We were bound by guilt, by the ropes of sins and habits that were taking us to a future away from God – ultimately to hell. We were so helpless that we didn't even know we *were* prisoners.

Then one day the picture changed. Someone had been praying for us, maybe someone befriended us, *and Christ walked over the bridge.* He came into the house of our lives, sliced through the bonds that held us prisoner and threw them away. He picked up a baseball bat in the corner and said 'See that intruder at the door? Take this and go and deal with him'.

We shrink back. 'Wouldn't it be better for *you* to go?'

'No, no – I've already dealt with him 2,000 years ago. He knows he's a beaten enemy. Now it's your turn to give him the push.'

And that, frankly, is what we do. Jesus is a liberator but he doesn't set us free *from* the fight. He sets us free *for* the fight. So, faced by pressure and temptation **we are to choose not to sin.** It is as simple and as inconvenient as that. The Devil (and he is a person – chapter 6) has power but his is a limited power against someone who has the Spirit of Christ living in them (1 John 4:4). He cannot make a believer sin, he only has power to entice and tempt. **If we do wrong it is because we have chosen to do so.**

We don't have to look for a new, massive infusion of spiritual power. All the power we need is given to us when Christ enters our life. What we do frequently lack is not power – but *motivation*. Half the time we don't even want to win – it is too personally inconvenient!

So the answer is: raise your motivation. We do this by gaining such a commanding picture of Christ – once crucified, now raised, ascended and finally returning in dazzling glory – that we *want* **to win this personal battle for his sake!** *Start* every day with the Bible. *Ask* every day that you may be filled with the Spirit. *Dedicate* yourself every day as Christ's faithful servant – and be a fighter! *Meet* regularly with the friends of Jesus around the Bible – and then *expect* to win.

Q.95

Why should Christians suffer?

Why is it that following Jesus seems in many quarters to be so unpopular? Is it inevitable that if we are Christians, then we must suffer?

Yes, it is. A Bible sentence to remember is Acts 14:22, where we read that Paul and Barnabas were 'strengthening the souls of the disciples... and saying that **through many tribulations we must enter the kingdom of God**'.

Once we are alert to this truth of essential Christian experience we find it everywhere. Then we wonder why we didn't see it before.

'Tribulations'

The Greek word is *thlipsis*. It means a confining, squeezing pressure. It can be used to describe pain (James 1:27), lack of stuff (2 Cor. 8:13) and a woman's labour pains (John 16:21). *It's used extensively of Christian suffering* (2 Cor. 2:4; 1 Peter 1:6). All through history the Christian church has faced the squeezing pressure of numerous enemies. We should expect that if we choose the way of Christ then life will be made uncomfortable for us by these enemies. It's something that needs to be taught to every new Christian.

'Must'

The *must* of Acts 14:22 above means it's **necessary**. The indication is that 'tribulation' is an essential part of following Jesus. 'In the world', said Jesus, 'you will have tribulation (*thlipsis*).' There are two reasons for this:

Firstly, because we are called to follow a man who was himself called to suffer. It is for his name's sake that we do so (Matt. 24:9; Luke 22:28,29).

Secondly, God has chosen the way of tribulation to help us grow spiritually (Rom. 5:3). It is natural for us to see setbacks as an unnecessary interruption – we hope that later we can get back to living a 'normal Christian life' – then we discover that coming across opposition *is* the normal Christian life. This adversity signals the 'nearness' of God's kingdom (Luke 21:25-28,31). The apostle Peter emphasises that the 'Way of the Cross', in other words living our lives in the face of the sort of opposition that Jesus suffered, is all part of the way of life for the believer (1 Peter 4:1,12,13).

'Enter'

The Christian and the unbelieving world see opposition and adversity from opposite viewpoints. To the world suffering is a dead end. To the Christian it is a gateway into personal growth and the very life of the kingdom. Strangely, and uniquely, the Christian world view sees 'suffering' and 'glory' as belonging together (1 Peter 5:1,10). The whole of Paul's two letters to the Corinthians is on the theme of *power through weakness*. The reason is that the Cross, despite looking like a moment of weakness, possesses the greatest power in all history.

'The Kingdom of God'

The kingdom is not a country, or land. It is the rule of God through the appointed king, Jesus Christ, in the lives of his subjects world-wide. It runs alongside all that is meant by *salvation*. 'The Kingdom of God is not a matter of eating and drinking **but of righteousness and peace and joy in the Holy Spirit**' (Rom. 14:17).

We need not seek suffering; yet suffering and the kingdom do go together (Rev. 1:9). *Why should they always go together?* Because the man of Galilee waves us over and says, 'I've been this way myself. Take up your cross and follow me.' – and millions have done just that.

FOR FURTHER STUDY: *The Stone that Became a Mountain*, Richard Bewes, Christian Focus Publications (see Ch. 9).

Q.96

How important is baptism?

I have become a Christian from another religion and I am nervous about being baptised – it could be a tension point for my family. How vital is it to be baptised?

First, welcome to the family of the Lord Jesus Christ. Every day, some 100,000 people become his followers, and every week some 1,600 new church congregations come into being. This is a great landmark for you at such a point in history!

The greatest problems in your life – your forgiveness, your relationship to God and your eternal destiny – were all solved the day you turned to Christ but there will naturally be a whole bundle of new problems facing you now. Others, who are now your sisters and brothers in Jesus Christ, feel for you and, no doubt, will pray for you. Here are some words of reassurance for you to think about as you think through the matter of baptism:

1. Christ has already saved you

Our salvation does not depend on whether we have been baptised. If that was the case Christianity would be a religion of salvation by what *we do* rather than *what God has done*. It is the death of Jesus that saves us and his 'Baptism of the Spirit' brought you into the company of all believers the day you were converted (1 Cor. 12:13). The day we say 'Yes' to Christ, we are assured of a place by his side, eternally, just like the thief beside Jesus on the Cross.

2. Christ is going to keep you

Having taken the great step of trusting Christ, you can take heart from the words of the apostle Peter to the persecuted believers of his time. He saw them as *'kept by the power of God through faith, unto salvation ready to be revealed in the last time'* (1 Peter 1:5 KJV). When the Lord Jesus Christ comes into our lives he is not going to forget us. If baptism looks like becoming a possibility he encourages us to 'Fear not, therefore; you are of more value than many sparrows. So everyone who acknowledges me before men, I also will acknowledge before my Father who is in heaven' (Matt. 10:31,32).

3. Christ is going to guide you

I'm sure you are praying about this question of baptism. If that is so then you can afford to relax a little over this issue because God knows about the timing and feasibility of taking this step. You should also stay in touch with the leaders of your Christian fellowship. As you and they pray you will start to feel settled as to what Christ is saying for you to do.

4. Christ is going to use you

A new thing has happened because Christ has come into your life. As far as your family is concerned *You* are now the key person. From now on – through your prayers, your own testimony of a changed life and perhaps one day through your baptism – others in your family may be enabled to turn to him who is 'the way, the truth and the life'.

My closing word of encouragement for you – Proverbs 16:7.

Q.97

Which church should I join?

I am a very new Christian. I think I should join a church – but which? Please give me some advice.

Welcome – that's wonderful. Wherever you now go you are a member of the biggest family of belief ever known; it is the *only* group to which Jesus Christ has personally pledged himself.

You are right to be thinking about 'the church'. The church is not a building, it is a spiritual company of those 'called out and summoned together' under the headship of Christ.

> But you are a chosen people, a royal priesthood, a holy nation, a people belonging to God, that you may declare the praises of him who called you out of darkness into his wonderful light (1 Peter 2:9 NIV).

The church, then, is to be the biggest thing in our life. Our membership within 'the Body of Christ' (to use one Bible description of the church) is going to colour and enhance all of our relationships, recreation and plans. Naturally this means that we need to discover which local part of the church Christ is calling us to join – the first thing to do is pray about it.

Here are the questions to ask yourself as you consider joining a church:

1. Does the Bible actually get opened here?

Try and find a church that really does take the Scriptures seriously, and preaches through them. Does it have small classes or groups that help new believers? At our own church we have a helpful course which has been shown to work, and is now available, internationally. It's called *Christianity Explored* (www.christianityexplored.com). It is equipped with handbooks and videos as required. The question to ask is 'Will I get fed spiritually, does the church provide a Bible diet?'

2. Is this the kind of church you could take an uncommitted friend to?
A vital question! It doesn't matter too much whether the church is lively or quiet, big or small, traditional or modern – *but is it real?* Does it feel welcoming? If so then it is likely to be a praying church. One that is looking outside itself and has not become a 'club'. Would you feel ashamed to take a friend along? Are they likely to hear a message that will help and challenge them?

3. Is there an authentic New Testament feel to the church?
Is it Trinitarian in its emphasis on the Father, Son and Holy Spirit as equally God? Is the saving death of Christ at its centre (1 Cor. 2:2)? Do the music and hymns reflect this? Are baptism and the Lord's Supper (Holy Communion) a proper part of the church order (these are the two 'sacraments' instituted by Jesus)?

4. On the whole, are the arrows pointing outwards from the church?
A Gospel fellowship will always be reaching out with the good news of Christ to service others in the community and be involved in worldwide mission. *Look to see if there is a meeting dedicated to prayer* – that is always a dead give-away as to where the ministry is directed.

We will never find a perfect church – simply because every church is composed of people like us – but Christ loves the church, and so must we.

Q.98

Why are Christians sometimes such a pain?

I have to tell you that I find non-Christian friends easier to get on with than my fellow-believers. Why is it that so often the non-Christians are nicer, more hard-working and sometimes even more honest than the Christians?

This really hurts and I'm afraid it's not a new problem. When he wrote to the Christians at Corinth, Paul was aware of their poor standards. God was undoubtedly in their lives, they could boast of spiritual abilities like speaking in tongues, yet they were grouped around rival factions (3:4,21). They also were spiritually pompous (4:6-21); were slack about sexual immorality (5:1,2); took each other to court (6:1-8); and failed over apostleship, marriage, women, money and even Holy Communion.

Paul wrote, 'I could not address you as spiritual, but as worldly – mere infants in Christ' (3:1). Again, 'You are still worldly. For since there is jealousy and quarrelling among you, are you not worldly? Are you not acting like mere men? (3:3).

That is the scandal – they were supposed to be followers of the purest person who ever lived yet they acted like 'mere men'.

But be thankful that we possess the two letters to the Corinthian church in the Bible because it demonstrates what an unpleasant bunch of people Christians can be when they (we?) have barely begun to experience the improving, sanctifying work of the Holy Spirit. Many of those among the Corinthians had been sexually immoral; idolaters; adulterers; men who practised homosexuality; thieves; greedy; drunkards; revilers and swindlers (1 Cor. 6:10). 'Such', Paul continues, **'were some of you'**.

Where were the 'nice' people that you mention? Presumably still outside the church because they sensed no need of salvation! Nice people are probably born, or brought up, nice – but it doesn't take away the fact of their rejection of God and their need of salvation.

In almost any church we join we shall be aware of the grumblers and the trouble-makers; the prickly and the angular; the mean and the greedy. No true New Testament church can possibly be completely pure because it should constantly be reaching out beyond its members. It is actually a healthy sign of evangelistic involvement in the community when a church has an untidy, and even unruly, 'fringe membership'. Better that, than to have a church that is so ultra-pure that it cannot make bridges to people outside its walls.

My challenge is this. Get into a house group or similar gathering organised by the church. For it's right there, in the enclosed confines of a small group, that we can really put into practice the New Testament principles of living as the church:

'**Put on then, as God's chosen ones, holy and beloved, compassion, kindness, humility, meekness and patience, bearing with one another and, if one has a complaint against another, forgiving each other; as the Lord has forgiven you, so you also must forgive. And above all these put on love, which binds everything together in perfect harmony**' (Col. 3:12-14).

You can't really do *that* on a Sunday. It's the smaller groups that are the workshop of practical Christianity.

One more challenge – what is it you really like about your non-Christian friends? Could it be that they don't place demands on you to become a better person? It's always easier to swim with the tide, than against it.

Q.99

How do I help the unbeliever to believe?

How do I help the friend who says that they would like to believe but that they simply can't?

Your friend's best prospect of becoming a believer in Christ may well rest, humanly speaking, on you. Nearly every time an individual responds to the good news of Jesus you will find that somewhere in the background was a friend. As Augustine said sixteen centuries ago, 'One loving spirit sets another on fire'.

Let us open this up a little.

1. Faith needs a background

In the days of the New Testament the background was the Jewish tradition, stretching back over centuries, expecting a Messiah. Today it is rather different, your friend may not have a religious framework for their thinking. Alternatively they may have a distorted religious world-view, such as that found in many New Age ideas.

A little undermining of their prejudices will be necessary and because you are their friend you can do this without offending them. A possible opener can be the challenge, 'Tell me what your world-view is?'. Everyone on Planet Earth has a world-view; what they believe about the meaning of life and the world as they find it – what's theirs? Explore it, probe it, question it and undermine it – all the time praying, '*Make him hungry, Lord, for truth*'.

2. Faith needs an event

We know, of course, that the search for faith is not a blind, empty search for just *anything*. It's more like the ancient search for the source of the River Nile.

Everybody knew that there must be a great lake where the mighty river started. It was just a question of keeping on looking for it.

The Christian has been given the latitude and longitude for the search for ultimate reality. We have a spiritual GPS system. We need look no further than the life, death and resurrection of the world's pivotal figure, Jesus Christ. In your discussions, keep coming back to *him*. The road to a living faith is the road that keeps Christ in view. 'Faith', wrote Os Guinness, 'does not feed on thin air, but on facts' (*Doubt,* Lion Publishing).

In the end, faith, for your friend, is not going to be a 'feeling' about Christianity but a rational and willing **response**.

3. Faith needs a trigger

'Who do you say that I am?' Jesus asked Peter. It was a trigger moment for the disciple but a trigger can equally be an event – an illness, the birth of a baby, a visit to church, the reading of a book, a death, a challenge from a friend. Keep looking for those opportunities that may help to tip your friend towards asking about the Kingdom.

It can take time. The singer, Garth Hewitt, once told a journalist *'My role is that of creating doubt in the mind of the ardent unbeliever'* but when that job is done, there will be openings for the electric 'trigger' moment.

Lord ...make him hungry for truth.

FOR FURTHER STUDY: *Christianity Explored*, Rico Tice and Barry Cooper, The Good Book Company. .

Q.100

Can I be a global Christian?

I am always travelling all over the world with my family. We do have a church at home but we cannot always be there. What's your advice, please?

You are so right in keeping the idea of your own church 'back at home'. There is no reason why you should not be in a home group or church Bible class even if your attendance is sporadic. If you are going to be away, you can always give other Christians your prayer requests and ask them for theirs. *Take your church membership seriously – and take it with you.*

The wonderful thing about your situation is that it will show you that you have not joined some cosy club but a world kingdom begun by none other than Jesus Christ. What is more, **you are now a travelling ambassador for this outfit.**

Yours is a privilege that does not come to many of us. Of course you have the high priority of your school work to consider but if you take a little care over it, you can also be a missionary.

The concern expressed in your question is a right one. It would be so easy to let all the ropes of your discipleship and church life slacken, little by little, but this need not be so. Carry your Bible on your person into every day and even if prayer is happening at strange times of day, let it be little and often.

Build up an international scrapbook of Christian contacts and churches worldwide. It will come together if you work at it. Gradually you can find your way in prayer around the family of Christ on different continents. Build up the names and addresses of people whom you can count on for fellowship, sharing Bible study and prayer support in different countries.

Become an international ambassador to these many contacts. How can you encourage *them*? What of the overseas churches that you visit – what are they short of? Can you take them something on your next visit? Some book gifts in your suitcase; something they can't easily get in the shops? As time goes by and you develop your prayer contacts and concerns it could be that you have *more than one home church* – your overseas visits will be eagerly looked forward to at both ends!

Begin as an international intercessor
Names, contacts, churches, problems; turn them all into prayer as you move around and don't forget to keep in touch with people back home. Thank God for e-mail and texts! See if, from time to time, you can give a report to your home church about where you've been to help them widen their horizons. You might even have something to bring back for *them* too! Ideas you have seen used in other youth groups; perspectives that we don't get from our culture. You are privileged, God bless you in it.

WORDS THAT CIRCLED THE WORLD

A Christian's response to 13 quotations that have shaped our times

RICHARD BEWES

'a rich blend of insight, sanity,
wisdom and humour'
John Stott

Words that Circled the World

A Christian response to 13 quotations that define our age

Richard Bewes

Richard Bewes weaves some of the best known quotes of our era into a remarkable book. Through these well known statements he is able to explore what motivates the modern mind and contrasts it with the wisdom of the Christian message. This unique book enables you to understand why the Christian faith is such a radical alternative in the post-modern world.

'He has a profound knowledge of Scripture, a close understanding of the contemporary world, and an uncanny knack of finding points of contact between the two. I warmly recommend it to anybody who wants to probe the basic issues of life. It is well conceived, well researched and well written. Readers will find in it, as I have done, a rich blend of insight, sanity, wisdom and humour, with Jesus Christ himself always at the centre.'

John Stott

The quotes included are -

'Yes, lady, God himself could not sink this ship' – deckhand on the Titanic

'I have in my hand a piece of paper' – Neville Chamberlain

'Power grows out of the barrel of a gun' – Chairman Mao Tse Tung

'I have a dream' – Martin Luther King

'I've been on a calendar, but never on time' – Marilyn Monroe

'I'd like to be a queen in people's hearts' – Diana, Princess of Wales

'I did not have sex with that woman' – President Bill Clinton

'To those who say that our city will never be the same I say, "You are right. It will be better"' – Mayor Rudi Guiliani

ISBN 1-85792-812-1

RICHARD BEWES

TALKING ABOUT PRAYER

'God bless you as you read this book.'
Billy Graham

Talking about Prayer

Richard Bewes

'I hope that this readable little book will find its way into the hands of Christian people on every continent, for it will have an immediate appeal to thousands who are rediscovering the life of prayer, both individually and through prayer groups.

Learn the secret of prayer! Through Christ we can find in God a heavenly Father, who hears and answers prayer. It is true to say that anyone who has ever advanced as a Christian and whose life counted for the kingdom of God has been a person of prayer.

It is my firm belief that Talking about Prayer could significantly strengthen the invisible network of praying people that God has brought into being around our world. God bless you as you read this book.'

Billy Graham

'I would never have chosen to write a book on the prayer life. What a subject – and how hypocritical one feels in making the attempt! This cannot be an exhaustive treatise; the very idea that anyone could cover the whole field of prayer in a kind of technical manual is ridiculous. But there might be some simple guidelines in these pages that can be put to use in your churches and fellowship groups. I have deliberately tried to let each chapter stand on its own, so that the reader can feel easy about dipping into the pages at random.'

Richard Bewes

ISBN 1-85792-613-7

BEGINNING
THE CHRISTIAN LIFE
RICHARD BEWES

*'I really don't think there is a better guide
to give to a new Christian'*
RICO TICE

Start

What Now?

Beginning the Christian Life

Richard Bewes

In this world 100,000 people a day are becoming Christians, in some countries the number outstrips the birth rate. Each week 1600 new congregations are formed.

This is not a story you will be familiar with through your news media!

Even in cynical Britain, for the ten years that straddled the 20th and 21st century divide, evangelical churches across all denominations saw an average 68% increase in regular attendees.

For you who have become one of those new believers, and also for those curious at such a phenomenon, Richard Bewes, the senior pastor of one of the largest churches in London, England, guides you into becoming a mature believer.

Richard is a regular broadcaster on BBC religious slots and a best-selling author but also his Anglican church has been one of those caught up in the amazing growth that occurs where people still teach the life-changing story of Jesus of Nazareth.

If you want to move forward in your life as a Christian start reading now!

'This book is full of humanity, colour and above all Bible wisdom. It wonderfully beckons us into a life of following Christ, and I really don't think there is a better guide to give to a new Christian'

Rico Tice, Author, Christianity Explored.

ISBN 1-84550-017-2

Christian Focus Publications

publishes books for all ages:

Our mission statement –

STAYING FAITHFUL

In dependence upon God we seek to help make his infallible word, the Bible, relevant. Our aim is to ensure that the Lord Jesus Christ is presented as the only hope to obtain forgiveness of sin, live a useful life and look forward to heaven with him.

REACHING OUT

Christ's last command requires us to reach out to our world with his gospel. We seek to help fulfill that by publishing books that point people towards Jesus and for them to develop a Christ-like maturity. We aim to equip all levels of readers for life, work ministry and mission.

Books in our adult range are published in three imprints.

Christian Heritage contains classic writings from the past.

Mentor focuses on books written at a level suitable for Bible College and seminary students, pastors, and other serious readers; the imprint includes commentaries, doctrinal studies, examination of current issues, and church history.

Christian Focus contains popular works including biographies, commentaries, basic doctrine, and Christian living. Our children's books are also published in this imprint.

Christian Focus Publications, Ltd
Geanies House, Fearn,
Ross-shire, IV20 1TW, Scotland,
United Kingdom
info@christianfocus.com
www.christianfocus.com